"Each one of these unique, personal, and vulnerable stories points to a bigger story: God's powerful story of calling, redemption, faithfulness, healing, provision, protection, and impact. You can't help being encouraged."
Dr. Steve Brown, president of Arrow Leadership, author of *Leading Me: Eight Key Practices for a Christian Leader's Most Important Assignment*

"If you need a reminder that your life is a magnificent masterpiece in which God is carefully crafting out your victory, you will want to read every word in this book. These stories will inspire you to write your own greatest chapters!"
Laura-Lynn Tyler Thompson, broadcaster, writer, politician, wife, and mother

"The Holy Spirit in the Hebrew language is referred to with feminine pronouns. I love that! I also love how these beautifully written stories will inspire confidence in all leaders. Men, this book gives insight into those women we work with. Women, you will be pushed to look beyond obstacles, face internal barriers, and change the world by helping other women to do the same. Read this book and learn from some of the best."
Rev. Dr. Carson Pue, executive mentor, author, speaker

"The inspiring stories of these women show how our God has his hand on our lives and is threading events, relationships, and opportunities into a beautiful handiwork for his glory and our good. Read and be encouraged."
Marilyn Gladu, member of Parliament, Sarnia-Lambton

"It is a special honour to endorse this book and the eight women telling their stories. This book will capture your attention, and you will seek to read it cover to cover in one read and then again chapter by chapter. Each woman tells her story of how God ensured that she was uniquely formed, impacted, influenced, called, equipped, compelled, encouraged, and empowered to lead in a sphere or context that matched who she had become. In every story obedience led to delivering national or international leadership beyond each woman's hopes, dreams, and anticipation. An awesome must-read for both women and men seeking to lead or already serving in leadership."
Paul Magnus, PhD, president emeritus, distinguished chair, professor of leadership, coach, consultant and facilitator, Briercrest College and Seminary

"Leadership can be very lonely at the top. The lie is that we can lead without other women to walk with us. That's why it's essential for leaders to invite mentors to join in their leadership journey. With over thirty years of experience leading alongside my pastor-husband in my family unit in my home, my skills were honed further in church and corporate positions. I've discovered we are not meant to lead any group alone. If you are a woman who leads a type of grouping, no matter the size or kind, you will find *Faith, Life and Leadership: 8 Canadian Women Tell Their Stories, Volume 2,* to be a valuable tool. The stories are those of real women leaders who struggled, pushed through, and gained ground to attain goals and with God's help strengthened and grew fruitful relationships within the groups they led. You don't have to lead alone anymore. Pick up two copies of this book, one for you and another for 'that other woman leader' who looks like she's got it all together. Invite her to coffee or tea and then share these stories of leadership as you share your own."

Sheryl Giesbrecht Turner, ThD, founder of From Ashes to Beauty, Inc.

"We all need authentic righteous role models. The apostle Paul says, 'Follow my example, as I follow the example of Christ' (1 Cor. 11:1). In *Faith, Life and Leadership: 8 Canadian Women Tell Their Stories, Volume 2,* I got to meet some remarkable Christ-loving role models. I say remarkable because the women candidly share their stories with perspectives, insights, and understanding that substantially testify to how they've pursued godliness in an ungodly world. If I were a younger woman looking to learn from the faith of older women (cf. Titus 2:3–5), this is one book I'd definitely read. But it's not just a book for younger women. I'm a middle-aged man who thoroughly enjoyed the inspirational, easy-to-read, warm, relatable stories!"

Dr. Lawson Murray, president of Scripture Union Canada

"I learned something from *Faith, Life & Leadership, Volume 1*: take time to listen with your eyes as each of eight 'ordinary extraordinary' women share their personal stories. Better prepared for *Volume 2*, I made a coffee for each chapter and savoured these eight new autobiographies one day at a time. The stories feature ordinary women, none with secret identities or a cape hidden in the closet, living the realities of life with extraordinary contributions because of a common thread—the Holy Spirit, 'the key to transformative and effective leadership development,' as Marg Gibb says. God inspired these women to inspire us. Enjoy!"

Don Hutchinson, principal of Ansero Services, former interim national director with Canadian Bible Society, and VP and director, Centre for Faith and Public Life with The Evangelical Fellowship of Canada

"I was moved as I lived the stories with the authors—rejoicing in their victories, hurting with them in their challenges. Memorable quotes will stick with me: 'Fear is a thief that robs us of opportunities,' 'Being always precedes doing,' 'When he calls, he equips,' 'Be unbending in the call ... be unashamed in your calling,' 'Lord, please let my life be lived, if not for income, then for outcome,' 'When you don't fear death, you don't fear life,' 'Leading is serving; serving is leading,' and 'Low ego/high trust.' These are powerful statements by powerful women. They are all as tough as nails, but as tender as new shoots—tenacious, but tender-hearted, living out God's call on their lives. Bravo!"

Honourable Deborah Grey, PC, OC, LLD

"Often in life, we see the success of others without knowing the process they have walked through to get to that point. In *Faith, Life, and Leadership: 8 Canadian Women Tell Their Stories, Volume 2*, we get a behind-the-scenes look into the lives of eight women who have not only weathered the storms but have also come out with nuggets of wisdom to share with those still in the process of becoming. If you feel stuck in your life, this book has biblical truths, mentoring wisdom, and fresh revelation to help break you through into a new place of faith, life, and leadership."

Saundra Dalton-Smith, MD, internal medicine physician and author of *Sacred Rest*

"Stories, more than instructional texts, have the power to connect not only with our intellect but with our heart and spirit. So it is with this inspiring book of sacred stories— the spiritual autobiographies of eight Canadian women of faith. What a fascinating group of women! Their backgrounds, life circumstances, gifts, and callings are diverse and utterly unique. What they share in common is deep faith, honest self-reflection, wise insight, and a hunger to be all that God intends for them. What makes this book compelling reading is to see and marvel at how God can take the raw materials of our lives—strengths, weaknesses, accomplishments, and failings—and fashion something beautiful and fruitful beyond our imagining."

Janet Clark, PhD, senior VP Academic, Tyndale University College and Seminary

Faith, Life AND Leadership

8 CANADIAN WOMEN TELL THEIR STORIES

Vol. 2

General Editor: Margaret Gibb
Foreword by Lorna Dueck

CASTLE QUAY BOOKS

Faith, Life and Leadership: Vol. 2—8 Canadian Women Tell Their Stories
Copyright ©2019 Margaret Gibb and Women Together
All rights reserved
Printed in Canada
International Standard Book Number 978-1-988928-15-9 soft cover
ISBN 978-1-988928-16-6 EPUB

Published by: Castle Quay Books
Tel: (416) 573-3249
E-mail: info@castlequaybooks.com | www.castlequaybooks.com

Edited by Natasha Lichti, Marina Hofman Willard, and Lori Mackay
Cover design and book interior by Burst Impressions
Printed in Canada

Library and Archives Canada Cataloguing in Publication

Title: Faith, life and leadership : 8 Canadian women tell their stories

Name: Gibb, Margaret, 1944- editor.
Description: Volume two edited by Margaret Gibb.
Identifiers: Canadiana 20169057984 | ISBN 9781988928159 (v. 2 ; softcover)

Subjects: LCSH: Leadership—Religious aspects—Christianity. | LCSH: Christian women—Religious life—Canada. | LCSH: Christian women—Canada—Biography. | LCSH: Christian biography—Canada.

Classification: LCC BV4597.53.L43 F35 2016 | DDC 248.8/43—dc23

CASTLE QUAY BOOKS

EDITOR

MARGARET GIBB is the executive director of Women Together, an international speaker, and a published author. Her extensive leadership experience includes 25 years of pastoral ministry with her late husband and 10 years as president of Women Alive. Since founding Women Together in 2011, Margaret has travelled the globe and expanded Women Together in nine countries. Her vision of building a global community of Christian women for mutual learning and sharing resonates internationally. A mentor, motivator and encourager, Margaret was selected as one of Canada's 100 Christian women leaders in 2014. She has two adult children, Tim and Tricia, who both serve in ministry in Canada and internationally.

CONTRIBUTORS

CHERYL WEBER, as a television host, public speaker, and senior executive producer of *100 Huntley Street*, is passionate about telling stories that matter. She has circled the globe documenting stories of human suffering, heartbreaking need, and incredible life transformation. Cheryl is the recipient of the Woman of Excellence Award for Raising Global Awareness and the International Women Achievers' Media Award. She serves on the board of Ratanak International, a Christian organization that empowers exploited people in Cambodia.

MOIRA BROWN is a Canadian television personality with more than 40 years of broadcast experience. She is best known for co-hosting *100 Huntley Street*, Canada's longest running daily TV talk show. In 2013, Moira was awarded the Queen Elizabeth II Diamond Jubilee Medal "for dedicated service to her peers, her community and to Canada." Moira is the author of *Hugs from Heaven: God's Embrace in the Adventure of Faith*, a collection of personal reflections on faith and life. Moira also shares her faith on Joy 1250 radio and at Faith Strong Today (faithstrongtoday.com).

LEILA SPRINGER is an author, a life coach, a breast cancer survivor, a community activist, and the founder and president of the Olive Branch of Hope Breast Cancer Support Services. She received an award for excellence in leadership from the World Conference on Breast Cancer Foundation, where she served as president for three years. Leila pursued her theological studies at Canada Christian College and Tyndale University College and Seminary. She creatively expresses her passion for God and the message of hope through public speaking and writing.

MARIE MILLER is a pastor, missions facilitator, itinerant evangelist, and the author of *Pray Simply and Simply Pray* (Castle Quay Books). She currently serves as lead pastor of Pickering Pentecostal Church. Before accepting the call to ministry, Marie worked in a marketing position at Air Canada. After witnessing extreme poverty on a trip to India, Marie quit her marketing job and enrolled in Bible college. She has since served on the pastoral teams of several churches and has ministered systemically in 29 countries under the banner of Foundations Ministries.

RUTH ANN ONLEY is an award-winning Christian recording artist who has touched hearts for over 30 years with her concert ministry. Married to David Onley, the 28th lieutenant governor of Ontario, Ruth Ann has had the opportunity to perform at many patriotic, military, and cultural events. Ruth Ann is the recipient of an honorary doctor of literature degree from Canada Christian College and the Queen Elizabeth II Diamond Jubilee Medal.

SUSAN FINLAY is the founder and national director of Nation At Prayer, a Canadian ministry focused on transforming the nation through prayer with and for elected representatives at every level of government. Before establishing Nation At Prayer, Susan worked as a senior consultant with an international consulting firm and enjoyed a fulfilling career in the government and not-for-profit sectors. Member emeritus and former board director of World Vision Canada, Susan has served on the boards of Tyndale University College and Seminary and an organization doing development work among women in Afghanistan. She is currently a mentor with Arrow Leadership.

WENDY HAGAR is the founder and executive director of Sew on Fire Ministries, a volunteer humanitarian organization that prepares and fills over 20,000 gift bags annually for people in need across Canada and around the world. Wendy began Sew on Fire from her home, but the ministry now works out of a 9,000 square foot distribution centre. Wendy is the recipient of Burlington's Citizen of the Year award and Queen Elizabeth II Diamond Jubilee Medal for her years of service.

AILEEN VAN GINKEL is vice-president of ministry services at the Evangelical Fellowship of Canada. She completed her doctor of ministry (DMin) degree in 2012 at Tyndale Seminary, where she focused her research on practices of communal discernment. Using her wide experience in facilitating group dialogue and collaboration, Aileen currently acts as a facilitator-coach with congregations and organizations that want to discern God's leading in ministry and mission. She and her husband, Edward, are parents to three children and live in King City, Ontario.

Faith, Life and Leadership: 8 Canadian Women Tell Their Stories is a project of:

WOMEN TOGETHER

www.women-together.org

Contents

Foreword

We are curious creatures, and I can't imagine life without that remarkable quality. To learn, to be amused, to succeed, to help or protect—it all begins with curiosity. The human race has always used stories to help guide the way through the psyche's curious nature. Stories set us at ease: they welcome us; they speak to us. The world's most popular book, the Bible, is a collection of stories. Real people, real situations, real encounters with an everlasting God all fill the pages of the sacred text.

I once had the privilege of sitting at the kitchen table of author Eugene Peterson to interview him about *The Message*, the easy-to-read vernacular version of the Bible that he had composed. Many millions of copies of *The Message* were in circulation at that time. With a patient draw of his breath and a gentle tapping of his fingers on the cover of *The Message*, Eugene said to me, "The Bible is a story ..." and then he proceeded to unfold examples of characters, plots, and literary styles that differ from story to story in the Bible. I've wondered ever since if we should not see the stories of our own lives quite differently. Could it be that God's Spirit is shaping each person available into the story God is writing? I do see the story of our lives that way. God's work in people didn't stop at the last page of the Bible's closing book, Revelation.

A friend of mine in media who is adept at story-telling and who is Catholic once asked of my evangelical Protestant tradition, "Why do you guys stop at the apostle Paul with your stories?" The question was referring to my personal passion to model my perseverance after the apostle Paul. I quoted Paul often as I battled through what I felt were obstacles worthy of comparison to shipwreck or stoning. Perturbed that the enduring validity of the apostle Paul's story might be challenged, I inquired more, and my friend, who had recently finished a meticulous documentation of Saint Jean de Brebeuf's story, challenged me to expand the variety of life stories that I reached into for God's lessons on perseverance.

God's work in the human race did not stop at the Bible. Every generation contains new truth of how the love of God can travel into the challenges of today. I think that's exactly what is underway in the collection of stories contained in this book. As you read these pages, you will learn that God is at work in your story also, that all the twists and turns of life are part of how God works divine purpose into our steps. God takes the details of each generation and weaves the mystery of the Holy Spirit into our activities because our lives matter to God's divine agenda.

"For we are God's handiwork, created in Christ Jesus to do good works, which God prepared in advance for us to do" says my favoured storyteller Paul in Ephesians 2:10. The handiwork of God, the good works, the road map of preparation that got a woman to good works—those are the stories in this book. As you discover these women, you will discover too how God has been working with your life for the good works prepared for you. Settle in for a good curious journey with the remarkable women in these pages.

Lorna Dueck, CEO, Crossroads Christian Communications and YES TV

Acknowledgements

How does a seasoned leader condense a lifetime of stories into 7,000 words? Where does one start? What should be included? What should be omitted? How does one clarify with words what was learned in the long and unpredictable development process?

The success of every book requires a writer, capable editors, and a committed publishing team.

Natasha Lichti did what gifted and capable editors do. As she edited words, sentences, and paragraphs, she guided the progression of each story but never altered the voice of the authors. Thank you, Natasha, for being a joyful writing coach.

Special thanks to our publishers, Larry and Marina Willard of Castle Quay Books, who continue to see the need for books that contain stories of life and leadership from influential Canadian women. Larry and Marina recognize that these stories serve as important mentoring tools for leaders on their journey. Thank you, Larry and Marina. Your encouragement spurs us on.

Margaret Gibb

Editor's Note

"Everyone has a story. Everyone's life is a story."
(Dan B. Allender)

Stories are powerful tools for communication. They touch the heart and define life in all its complexity and vast possibilities. Stories help us to view reality and teach us how to properly respond to life and its challenges. Stories have the power to transform us and help us to find—and be anchored in—our God-given purpose. Stories instill hope.

The eight contributors chosen for this second volume of *Faith, Life and Leadership* were selected for the diversity of their professions and experiences. Although their journeys of faith, life, and leadership are different, they all possess a deep awareness of calling and a spirit of perseverance to ride out the tough times. Like all of us, each of the authors faced the unpredictability of life in the face of the unknown, and we see that their stories were made richer as they grew in knowledge and wisdom.

With frank openness, the authors describe their inner battles with fear, inadequacy, and harbouring pain and offences. Their determination to step out of comfort zones to reach higher in faith, accomplishment, and character development provides a model of leadership. These women inspire readers to believe they can overcome because God's grace will work to fulfill his purposes in the lives of all women.

All of the contributors in this book see the events in their lives not as a coincidence or as a streak of luck but as part of a sacred journey, a walk with the God who created them and who continues to lead through unimaginable circumstances.

Stories connect us together—author and reader. Sharing stories gives us imagery. It transports us to another place, and more often than not we see ourselves in the story. I pray that you, our reader, are inspired as you immerse yourself in the amazing stories of eight Canadian leaders who lived with unwavering faith and watched God transform the impossible into possible.

Margaret Gibb

Dreaming God's Dreams

Cheryl Weber

I t was early morning in the fall of 2002, and I was getting ready for a TV shoot. As I sat on the edge of the bed, I heard God whisper quietly to my heart, "You are living your dream." I was floored. I was three months into my new job as a national reporter for *100 Huntley Street*, but I had yet to realize that this was a significant dream fulfilled. How had that been possible? As I reflected, I realized that I had laid this dream down so many times at God's feet, praying for his will to be done in my life, that I had literally forgotten about it.

Tears flooded my eyes as I reflected on the absolute faithfulness of God. Though I had long ago given up on this dream, he had never forgotten. My journey to this point in my life was winding, surprising, and sacrificial. But the lesson of exchanging my desires for his has been the bedrock of my journey. God asks us to give our lives, desires, and dreams to him. And then he writes a story we could never have imagined.

DECIDING TO FOLLOW JESUS

I cannot tell my story without including many instances of God speaking to me, either personally or through someone else. It is my sincere belief and experience that God still speaks today, and his words have been the foundation of my life and ministry. God's words have rarely been revealed to me in an audible or overwhelming manner. Instead, God has spoken to me through a thought that came to life out of the blue—quiet, unassuming, and peace-filled.

When I started my faith journey at the young age of four, I could never have imagined all that God had for me. I had watched my parents give their lives to God, and I knew that they had something real. They were changing—becoming more loving, kind, and peace-filled. I wanted what they had. So I prayed a simple prayer and asked God to come into my life and heart.

Soon my parents experienced what they called being "Spirit-filled" after inviting the Holy Spirit to fill them completely. I saw more changes. I wanted to experience this too, but my parents believed I was too young. I was incredibly persistent, not wanting to miss out on anything this new relationship with God could give me. Finally, I wore my parents down, and they agreed to pray with me. It was a day I remember as clearly as if it happened yesterday. We prayed together, and when I closed my eyes, I saw a swirling ball of colour go right into my belly. My entire being filled with warmth, and I asked my family to sing "Jesus Loves Me." The decision to accept the Holy Spirit changed me. My mom reports that I stopped fighting frequently with my sister. Moving forward with God should produce change!

My parents were so fiercely hungry to know more about God that we were in a different kind of church service many days of the week. I experienced the Catholic Charismatic Movement, the Jesus Movement, Full Gospel Businessmen meetings, Women's Aglow meetings, and a variety of other charismatic renewal meetings. In the weekly prayer meetings that my parents led, I would often enclose my tiny offering with a piece of paper on which I'd write, "I give myself to God." It was the innocent act of a small child, but I know now that God took me very seriously.

At the same time that I was experiencing the charismatic renewal, I was also attending the Lutheran church in which I grew up. I attended Trinity Lutheran Church until I was 19 years old; my first communion and confirmation were held there. I had a Heinz 57 faith: attending Presbyterian Sunday school with friends, Catholic funerals, and Pentecostal youth groups and following my parents' lay preaching into every evangelical church imaginable. Little did I realize that this early exposure would lay the foundation for my ministry today where I work with every possible Christian denomination. I see the truth of the words of Psalm 139:16: "You saw me before I was born ... Every moment was laid out before a single day had passed" (NLT). God was orchestrating my path before I could even see it.

During those intense years of literally growing up in church, many people prayed with me, and a theme emerged: they saw a call on my life to international ministry, which became woven into the fabric of my mind and heart. I cannot remember many of the individual moments that built this certainty, but it became engraved into my identity.

SURRENDERING TO GOD'S PERSISTENT CALL

Despite the certainty of my ministry calling, I didn't always follow the path of purity. As a teenager, I had a rebellious streak. I wanted to experience and explore life in every way. God was always real to me, but like so many teens, I felt I had time to experiment before I started living by the tenets of my faith. For now, I wanted to find out if everyone was having as much fun as they seemed.

Curiosity led to a party lifestyle that was augmented by the influence of my boyfriend. I made some bad choices over those years. I know with a great degree of certainty that my parents' prayers are likely the only reason I escaped without injury or severe consequence. Although my lifestyle was far from God, he never left me. I began to experience a reoccurring phenomenon: when I was in bars, I would hear someone calling my name audibly from far away. But no one was there. I eventually acknowledged that this was likely God calling me home. I remember one poignant experience on a train where God began to speak to me about coming back to him. I wanted to say yes, but I felt trapped by the relationship I was in. To return to God would mean giving up the boy I loved. I wept with lonely tears at my inability to say yes.

Although the heartfelt prayers of my parents didn't seem to be making headway into my rebellious lifestyle, God was working a much bigger plan for me. My father talked to me about the chance to visit Oral Roberts University—a Christian university in Tulsa, Oklahoma—for a weekend. For some reason, I agreed to the visit. When I went there, I knew immediately this was the university I was called to attend. It's hard to explain how a lost girl could sense this, but although my lifestyle was far from God, he still owned my heart. I might have lived a life of sin temporarily, but I wasn't about to mess with the overall calling of my life.

The decision to attend Oral Roberts caused a lot of friction with my boyfriend, who didn't understand my reasoning. But I was adamant. I knew I had to go. Upon arriving on campus my freshman year, I was given a job in the library to help me pay for school. My new boss turned out to be a marriage counsellor, and he immediately began forcing me to face some unpleasant realities about my relationship. He wanted to know how I would raise my kids with a man who didn't share my faith. He asked me what God was saying about the relationship. It was annoying!

By the time I headed home for my fall break, things with my boyfriend were tenuous. When I met with him, something supernatural happened. I saw clearly that if I continued to pursue this relationship, I would never fulfill the calling on my life. It was as if God set out two choices before me: life or death. I couldn't give up on all that God had for me. Somehow I ended the relationship. It was one of the hardest things I've ever done. But as time and experience revealed, it was a decision I thank God for helping me make. It changed the trajectory of my life. Throwing away your destiny for anything or anyone on this earth is never worthwhile.

AN UNLIKELY MEDIA PERSONALITY

I went to university as a piano major but soon discovered that my love of music was a relaxing hobby, not a full-time pursuit. I signed up for courses in business management, counselling, and introduction to media. It was in the latter course that my heart and imagination were set on fire. The instructor used studies and stories to show the impact of media on society's thoughts and actions. He challenged us to think about how we could harness that to inspire people to faith. My course was set. I threw myself into my studies, despite being so terrified of appearing on camera that I would have a near panic attack just from sitting in a chair where students would practice camera focus.

I was so painfully shy that my university roommate, Janine, would introduce me as "Cheryl, my silent roommate." When my mother shared with her that God had told her I was going to be a media personality, Janine fell off her chair in gales of laughter. But God sees things in us that we can't even imagine. I've learned that he always speaks to our potential, not our reality. Years later when Janine visited me as I was reporting nationally for *100 Huntley Street*, she said, "Who *are* you?" God had done a deep work in my life over the years as I stepped into areas that intimidated me.

I decided a long time ago to not let fear dictate my decisions or my life. Fear is a thief that robs us of opportunity, vision, and destiny. It causes us to miss out on so many amazing experiences that life holds. While it may be uncomfortable to face our fears, I've learned that fear is a bully. If you stand up to it, it *will* back down. Every step I've taken in my career or life has been intimidating. I've often felt unqualified or unworthy, but I refuse to let those feelings dictate my actions. I don't want to miss one thing that God has planned for me because I said "no." Those voices of discouragement and fear do not come from God.

I persisted in my studies, focusing on broadcast journalism, despite my fear of appearing on camera. I hosted our campus news show and interned as a radio reporter for an all-news radio station. I remember praying that I would see a dead body in my reporting so that I could endure the trauma as an intern and not mess up my reporting when it counted. I never did. I would always arrive just as the ambulance was pulling away. I see now that God protected me. That was not a skill I needed to develop!

One of my most memorable days as a radio news intern happened when the police invited the news crew along on a drug bust one early morning. The police told us to stay in our cars, but the reporter I was shadowing stealthily followed them. My job was to follow the reporter, so I did! Picture the scene with me: I was in a skirt, a silver alligator raincoat, and heels, ducking down below the window of the house the police were assaulting. I had a moment of doubt as I spotted the gun underneath the windbreaker of the policeman in front of me. But it was too late. The police were pounding on the front door, and we were following as they cleared the house. The reporter acquired some powerful audio as I watched the police throw the homeowner on the floor and frisk her. The drug dealer was not home, and the poor woman was hysterical. When I related the adventure to my professor and later my parents, their reaction was not as positive as I'd hoped. The reporter had risked an intern's life for a story? They were not impressed, but I loved it.

WAITING FOR GOD'S GIFT TO OPEN A DOOR

When I graduated, I was voted "the most likely to succeed in broadcast journalism." I literally went from being the least likely person to receive that award to having my peers vote for me! It had to be God. So, it was humbling to return home to a broadcast industry that had been gutted by a bad economy. The main television station in my hometown of Windsor, Ontario, was being closed down, and seasoned reporters were fighting for the jobs that were left. There was not much hope for a recent graduate.

I took a summer job in a pick-your-own strawberry field, which was incredibly disheartening. I kept looking for work, sticking to secular job opportunities. I wanted to work in *real* television, not what I considered to be cheesy Christian TV. I heard from my father that David Mainse, host of *100 Huntley Street* and founder of Crossroads Christian Communications, was coming to town for a banquet. Because my father was helping to organize the event, he asked David's producer if I could help in any way. I was not familiar with the show, because we didn't receive it in Windsor, but I was assured that it was high-quality television—not like the Christian television I had judged so harshly. My dad arranged for me to help the team from Crossroads, and somehow I ended up at a pastors' luncheon sitting with David Mainse. It was incredibly intimidating for a shy 23-year-old. David asked me to drive him around and shared with me some ideas he had for a media series. He suggested that perhaps I could write the series if the opportunity arose.

When the team returned to Crossroads, every person I had met tried to get me a job there—including David Mainse. The only openings at the time were a job phoning partners and a secretarial position. I had been encouraged in school to take any job to get my foot in the door because the media industry works on word of mouth. I visited the station, and, after many conversations, tests, and interviews, I accepted the position of executive secretary to the vice-president of development. But my excitement soon dimmed as over the course of that year I began to feel stereotyped as only a secretary. No one seemed to see or understand that I had other aspirations. I felt boxed in, not only by others' thoughts of me but also by my gender. It felt at times that many held the opinion that women should hold only service-oriented positions, not leadership roles. Whether that was true or not, I cannot say. But that was my perception at the time. However, I had much bigger dreams.

It was in the midst of that frustration that I heard God whisper clearly to my heart. He reminded me of the proverb in Proverbs 18:16: "A man's gift makes room for him, And brings him before great men" (NKJV). I sensed that God was assuring me that it didn't matter what anyone thought of my gifts, my talents, my gender, or my potential. The gift he had placed in me would open doors. God told me to hold on to that truth, no matter what my circumstances looked like. It was the best advice I could have been given. Over the years, through both highs and lows, I have clung to this verse. I believe that God has placed unique gifts in all of us that—if stewarded well—will open doors. Many times these doors are bigger than we would ever dream of for ourselves. That was certainly the case for me.

Soon I began to have opportunities to write, and I was offered a position in another area of the ministry to help develop a parent-child magazine. This was followed by jobs doing graphic design, producing a parent-child newsletter, and being an associate producer for children's television. I threw myself wholeheartedly into every new position that God brought my way, believing that each new area must be my calling. My goal-oriented, highly focused self could not imagine why else God would have opened the door. But as my job kept changing, I began to realize that I hadn't reached my final destination. Each new job was part of my training. And the training wasn't just about the job skills I was learning but about other life skills I would need for the journey.

I'm reminded of the famous scene in the movie *The Karate Kid* where the teacher, Miyagi, makes the kid, Daniel, perform laborious chores, such as waxing his car. Daniel is frustrated with being taken advantage of, not realizing that all of the movements in his chores are training him in martial arts moves. I think God often trains us in this way. We don't understand the season we are in or why we are going through hardship, but in hindsight we realize God was preparing us for a season yet to come. I learned valuable leadership and interpersonal skills in this time, and I grew in experience and confidence.

LAYING DOWN MY DREAMS TO MAKE ROOM FOR GOD'S PLAN

Early in my career I learned to be a producer, which is mainly behind-the-scenes work. I produced children's television, radio shows, and a church television show, leaving Crossroads to work with other ministries. None of this involved journalism or being in front of the camera. As each door opened, I progressively laid down my dream of being an international reporter. God did not seem to be opening those doors. I prayed to submit to whatever narrative he was writing for me, no matter what it was. The dream died.

Through many years now of following God, I have learned that the death of a dream is often an important part of God fulfilling it. Once you die to it, it is no longer your dream. If he resurrects it, then it will be his dream. Your ownership and possession of it are over. I believe this was an important part of the journey he had me on. One thing I have learned: when you fight and politick for your dream, then you are the one who also has to maintain and defend it against others who want it. It can be exhausting. But when God opens a door and it is his dream, then it is his job to defend it. You know you will only have it until the day he decides you must move on. And since you have submitted to his will for your life, you always have to hold on to your dreams loosely. It is his story he is writing. I have found great freedom in this, although it is a discipline of the heart to maintain that stance.

God in his great kindness was still speaking to me about my dream of international reporting even when all doors seemed closed. I clearly remember a friend from church, who had a very keen gift of hearing from God, telling me that she had had a vision of me reporting in front of Canada's Parliament. It stumped me. I was already in my 30s, and in my opinion, I was not television material. In order to become a national reporter who would do that kind of story, you needed to work in cable news, local news, and then eventually national news. It was already too late for me to achieve that goal. I wrote the vision in my journal and said, "God, if this is from you, then I trust you to make it happen in your time."

TRUSTING GOD THROUGH A SEASON OF SUFFERING

After hearing about my friend's vision, I heard a man speak in my church who had a unique relationship with God. Everything he said seemed to have a freshness to it that came from his daily conversations with God, along with reading Scripture. It was challenging my faith in very foundational ways, and it caused me to pray what I call a "dangerous prayer." I said, "God, I want to know you as you really are. Not as I think you are, or as I'm comfortable with you being, or as I've been taught that you are. I want to know *you*." Little did I know that this prayer was about to change my life … again.

I grew up with a theology that strongly emphasized faith, and I genuinely believed that my destiny would only involve health and wealth. I had no room in it for suffering. When I prayed to know who God really is, I believe God knew I was missing a huge piece of what it means to follow him. All these years later, I have realized that I have a call on my life to be a voice for the oppressed, and yet I had no idea at that time how God viewed suffering. It wasn't long after that prayer that I lost everything—my job, my car, my pets, my best friend, my home—even my ability to walk (as I suffered a traumatic break in my ankle).

I like to call this time of my life my "Job season," named after a man in the Bible who lost everything. There is much to learn from him. Going through a season of suffering when you have no theology to explain it is an incredibly painful experience. How could I trust a God who would take everything from me? I had been serving a God who was predictable. "If I do this, then he will do that" was the foundation of my belief. Suddenly God was unpredictable, and I was frightened by this side of him. How was I to trust him if he could allow something so painful to happen to me? These questions affected me for many years.

During this humiliating time of moving back in with my parents in Windsor, Ontario, after a decade of being on my own, God connected me with some wise and prayerful older women. We began to meet to pray about some of the past wounds of my life. This launched an uncomfortable 10 months of facing my pain, wounds, and fears. I believe God allowed me to be broken in this season so that I would deal with the core issues in my life. We do not easily face our own pain, but the level of loss in my life opened the door to deep soul-searching. It's true that hurt people hurt people. Through counselling and prayer, I began to learn new life skills, such as standing up for myself and getting in better touch with my feelings. Healing was coming. I couldn't see the changes in myself during the process, but over the next few years I realized I was responding differently to situations similar to those I'd faced in the past. God had done a deep work in me.

I genuinely believe that good leadership is built on the foundation of self-awareness, counselling, and continual heart restoration, which is only possible through God. If leaders do not invest in their own emotional health, then their areas of weakness will cause pain in those they are leading. It's not a one-time effort. It's a continual process of praying along with King David in Psalm 139:23–24: "Search me, O God, and know my heart; test me and know my anxious thoughts. Point out anything in me that offends you, and lead me along the path of everlasting life" (NLT). At different seasons in my life, I have sought out either professional counselling or spiritual prayer and healing. Each instance has catapulted me into new freedom, opportunities, and peace.

A HEART FOR THE NATIONS

During my time of unemployment, I felt that God was clearly telling me *not* to look for work, because he would open a door without any help from me. Ten months had gone by, and my bills were piling up. I was depressed and living with my parents without a car or even money to buy myself a coffee. I wondered if I was really hearing from God correctly.

Out of the blue, just as God had said, I received a job offer in the spring of 1998 from a friend's production company in Burlington, Ontario. I was asked to produce a journalistic-style television show for Canadian evangelist Bill Prankard. This opportunity was meaningful for me because years before I had heard Bill speak at a church service about his work, and I had told God that I would love to work with him someday. I had forgotten about my prayer, but God never did. Bill's ministry worked in remote areas of the earth, and I had a strong desire to go shoot these stories. That was another change in me that happened because of one moment of surrender during an unusual church service.

I had always been a homebody, asking my friends to come to my house instead of visiting theirs. Although I knew I had a global calling, the idea of roughing it never appealed. Quite frankly, it scared me! I was hoping that God intended me to do beach ministry from five-star resorts.

In the mid-1990s, I listened to a speaker in church who was talking about those who felt called to go to the nations. He challenged us to walk up to the front of the church if we had that calling. I sat in my chair, wrestling. I hated the idea of standing up in front of everyone, and

I reasoned that I could talk to God about it right where I was sitting. But the draw to stand up and acknowledge it wouldn't leave me. I slowly walked to the front of the church as the speaker told us to take off our shoes and commit our feet to God. I heard God whisper to me, "Dusty corners of the earth, remote areas where no one goes," and I began to sob from deep within. I didn't want to go to these places, but I knew that God was calling me. I took off my shoes in obedience and said, "I will go wherever you want, but one thing I ask of you: change my heart so that I have a desire to do these things. I don't want to do them with a resentful attitude." I went home that night exhausted but strangely at peace. A battle had been won.

I really enjoyed producing Bill Prankard's program *Sea to Sea*. I never travelled to the places he ministered in, but I was able to produce many impactful stories from the Far North. After a year of working with Bill, he let the production company I was working with know that he was going to produce the show in-house. It looked like my job would soon end. However, in that same month, in 1999, a new job opened up back at Crossroads Christian Communications. I had never intended to return, but the draw of finally getting back to journalism and producing Lorna Dueck's news show *Listen Up* was too much to resist. During the summer of 2000, I took a break from *Listen Up* to produce various shows for Crossroads at the World's Expo in Frankfurt, Germany. That summer in Europe was one of the best in my life. At the end of my time, I bought a Eurorail pass and backpacked with a friend through five European countries. In the process, I fell in love with world travel, roughing it on trains, in two-star hotels, and in hostels. God had completely changed my heart.

By the time I returned to Canada, I was barraging heaven with prayers to travel—or even live—internationally. Now that God had changed my heart, I could hardly wait to get going. I had a new thirst for adventure to go with my long-held passion for justice work, but doors were not opening. As a matter of fact, for most of the next decade, as I worked with both *Listen Up* and eventually *100 Huntley Street*, our senior producer was adamant that the purpose of these shows was to cover Canadian stories and that international stories were outside of our mandate. I tried to convince him that part of our Canadian identity was that we were citizens of the world, but to no avail. Thankfully, he did allow a few international trips, which helped me keep the faith. But I'm getting ahead of myself.

LEARNING TO TRUST IN GOD'S FAITHFULNESS

During a trip to Washington, DC, to cover a global HIV/AIDS conference, Lorna Dueck asked for either myself or my co-producer, Denise Lodde Roberts, to report on camera for *Listen Up*. By this time, I was quite comfortable behind the scenes and didn't think I was "on-camera material." So I asked Denise to appear on camera. She did a tremendous job! But God needed to deal with my heart to make me willing to do on-camera work. He worked on me in many ways over that summer. I was passionate about having my own voice, and I found that as a producer, it often wasn't getting through.

By September of 2003, Lorna Dueck had decided to leave her position as host of *100 Huntley Street*, and the future of *Listen Up* was unsure. I was praying deeply about my future, worried about being unemployed once again. During that time, God gave me many assurances of new opportunities opening up before me. And again, he was right. I was offered the opportunity to lead a team of reporters nationally on *100 Huntley Street*. This opportunity had me leafing through the pages of my journal to find a promise God had given me two years before. He had told me he would give me a leadership position with *100 Huntley Street* that would be very creative. I wasn't sure at the time I was hearing God correctly, but I followed my habit of writing it down anyway in case I needed to look back on it in the future.

Journaling has been one of the most faith-building habits I've formed. It amazes me how those quiet "God thoughts" really do turn out to be his leading. I still had doubts about whether I was "on-camera material," but my new boss was confident in me, which helped a lot. I accepted the position and was immediately reporting at a national level, skipping all the intern steps I believed had to happen. It was humbling to learn how to report before a national audience, but because I knew that God had opened the door, I walked through it.

For the next three years, I'm pretty sure I didn't sleep during the nights before appearing on air. I was intimidated but determined to press on, despite my fears. God had revealed to one of my friends that I was wearing shoes that were too big for me but that I would grow into them. And I did. One of the stories that I produced in those first months was in Ottawa. As I was doing a night stand up in front of the parliament buildings, God reminded me of the vision my friend had had years ago.

I was reporting nationally, just as God had said. He is faithful even when we don't believe. I have also observed that God delights in throwing us in over our heads. It's at times like these that we depend on him completely. We are desperate, we are aware of our need of him, and we do not rely on ourselves. He loves it when we are in this place. The truth is that this is how we should always function, but our humanity causes us to seek confidence and comfort in everything *but* him.

If you take away one thing from my story, I hope it is that God still speaks today. His voice, vision, and direction are key to good leadership. When I was a young girl, my parents taught me how to hear God's voice. They would send me off with a piece of paper and a pen and tell me to do four things. One: ask God to forgive my sins and forgive others for hurting me. Two: sing a song or two of praise to God. Three: read the Bible. Four: ask God to speak, and wait, listen, and write down what I heard. I would come back with simple words, such as "I love you, Cheryl." I would show them to my parents, who would affirm that that was indeed God's voice. It was childlike, but that instruction set me up for life. I am so thankful for this early training. It's not always easy to be 100 percent sure that you are hearing God's voice, but I've committed to write down what I think I'm hearing. Often it doesn't require action, just a simple faith to say, "If this is you, God, show me." And he does. My journals are an enduring record of his faithfulness.

A TASTE OF INTERNATIONAL REPORTING

Speaking of God's faithfulness, in 2004 I finally took my first international trip as a reporter, to Cuba. I had the opportunity to go undercover to expose the poverty that Cubans lived under, despite the government's propaganda. I had made a connection with a man who was helping Canadians visit Cuba with the secret purpose of bringing aid to the interior, where tourists never visited. It was an amazing trip—seeing cowboys on horses, living with Cubans in impoverished conditions, worshipping in a church where people were so poor they wore their pyjamas to the services, following horses and carriages down to a lake at night to witness a baptism, and being deeply touched by the Cubans' bold faith in difficult circumstances. It was my first experience witnessing extreme poverty, and it shattered me.

I remember one of my co-workers sharing with me the difficulty of not being able to talk about all we were witnessing. There were informants everywhere in the communist nation, and we didn't want to risk the undercover work that was being done by our new friends. After our conversation, I was feeling disheartened and began to pray. God showed me a picture of a flower slowly opening up and told me that I was made for this. It would be a few years before I fully understood what he meant.

In my early days of reporting, I spent some time volunteering with the International Justice Mission (IJM) as it was launching in Canada. International Justice Mission's Canadian executive director, Jaimie McIntosh, gave me a DVD of a *Dateline NBC* special called "Kids for Sale." It documented the overt sale of young children for sex in a small town outside of Phnom Penh, Cambodia. I had never seen anything so horrifying in my life. I wept as I watched little girls pitch sex acts to North American men. My stomach turned and I fought nausea for nearly a week as I remembered what I had seen. I began to pray three things for the girls I had seen in the video: that they would be rescued, that they would come to know God, and that they would be healed.

Jaimie McIntosh called me one day to alert me to a story developing in Canada: a man had been caught torturing a sex trade worker in a public park, and in their investigation the Vancouver police had found videos of the man assaulting children in Asia. Through what I can only describe as an act of God, the police were able to get the exact GPS coordinates of the assault in Cambodia within 48 hours, thanks to the help of IJM and another Christian organization in Canada, Ratanak International. I was able to document the first sex tourism conviction in Canadian history, a story that deeply impacted me.

GOD'S PLANS ARE ALWAYS BETTER THAN OUR DREAMS

Not long after covering the sex tourism story, I was asked to share a little bit of my story at a church in Toronto. While I was waiting to be called up on stage, a couple behind me shared that they had seen me on television that morning. They were from the US and didn't know anything about me, but they felt led to pray for me. I immediately agreed. I love being prayed for! I don't remember what the couple said, but as they began to pray, a deep grief came over me from out of the blue, and I began to weep and cry out silently to God. I was begging him to give me an opportunity to help little girls who were trafficked for sex. I do not know where this desire came from. I was not thinking about it at all. I believe this was something supernatural that God was depositing in my heart.

In the meantime, I had produced a number of stories on Ratanak International and its founder, Brian McConaghy, who had become a good friend. We had talked many times about getting me to Cambodia to tell stories of how God was transforming girls who had been trafficked. Brian and I must have come up with a plan to make this happen at least three times. The idea was that I would use my vacation time and volunteer to produce the story, but each time the plan fell through. The last time we tried to plan the trip, Brian's board even approved a budget, but then circumstances changed. Brian and I often wondered why we couldn't make this trip happen.

Finally, I pitched the story in 2009 to the director of Crossroads Relief and Development, David Shelley. I told him about the work of Ratanak International in Cambodia and how Brian would allow us unprecedented access to the story because he trusted me to follow his directives to protect the girls. David agreed to meet with Brian, and soon I was on my way to Cambodia.

If the trip had happened any of the other times I had tried to make it happen, it would only have had a fraction of the impact. Not only had Crossroads agreed to partner with Ratanak International to help this work, but we were able to raise more than $600,000 for both Ratanak International and IJM to fight sex trafficking. But God's blessings did not stop there. Remember my prayers for the girls featured in the *Dateline NBC* documentary? I was able to personally meet many of those same girls and sit across from answered prayers: they were rescued, they had a relationship with God, and they were on a journey of healing. I was deeply touched by the absolute kindness of God in allowing me to see that he not only heard my prayers but arranged for me to see in person his answer to them. There's a lesson for all of us in this: when you see something on the news and you pray for God's help, *he hears*. You are praying his heart. He is full of compassion and kindness. Don't ever believe that prayer is a waste of time. God went very far out of his way to demonstrate this to me.

The most important lesson of that trip was that when God says no, he has a good reason for it. When he denies us the desires of our hearts, it may seem as if he is being unkind. But the truth of the matter was that he had a much better plan for me. And by waiting, I was able to receive blessings I could never have imagined. I see people fighting all the time for their destiny, their platform, or their ministry. My biggest lesson is that by allowing God to be the one who opens the door, I can rest from the entire struggle. He is trustworthy. He will accomplish everything he has promised for you, if you will just let him. A dream fulfilled out of its season is diminished from what God could do if we let him.

DEVELOPING A THEOLOGY OF SUFFERING

My dream of reporting internationally came true, even during the years of closed doors. In 2005, I was able to travel to India with the Voice of the Martyrs to report on the persecution of Christians. I asked God during those weeks to give me a theology of suffering. I felt a call to be a voice for the voiceless, but I had much to learn about how God viewed their pain.

During my trip, I was asked to speak to an impoverished church. At first, I did not want to say yes. I was not there on a mission trip but as a journalist to report on a story. The first lesson of journalism is objectivity. You cannot enter the story—you are there to report it. However, I wanted to be open to God's leading, so I took the five minutes I had to prepare to ask God for something to say. He gave me a powerful picture, telling me that India was a very hard place to live. It had spiritual darkness and deep poverty. Added to that was the persecution Christians experienced. God told me that I was about to meet a people whom he had honoured with suffering and whom he trusted. He knew that no matter what they faced, they would remain faithful to him.

I became emotional as the impact of what God was saying washed over me. By the time I stood up in the church to speak, I could not deliver his words without tears. Afterwards, knowing that these people were Dalits, considered untouchable by their neighbours and the lowest of the low, I made a point of laying my hand on each of the women and praying for them. In God's eyes, they were *not* untouchable, and I wanted them to know it.

This was a big step in my education on suffering that began during my "Job experience," and my education continued as I tried to process these lessons over the years. I had to learn how God viewed suffering and how to trust him in difficult seasons. It was in his kindness that he began to educate me. I could not speak about something I had never experienced.

I remember producing a story on a woman who had been healed of breast cancer. Although she had been healed, by the time the surgeon realized it, he had mangled her breast. As she told me the story, I tried to comfort her by saying that God could still restore her breast. But in my heart I immediately felt that this was wrong. God spoke two words to me: "battle scars." He sounded very proud of her. I didn't understand what he meant. A few weeks later, I was looking through footage of a church service where Canadian evangelists Bill and Gwen Prankard were speaking. All of a sudden, I saw tire tracks down their bodies. I asked God what it meant. He told me it was the price they had paid to take the message of Jesus across Canada all these years. And he proudly said, "battle scars." I was beginning to get the picture. Not long after that, my pastor was talking to me, and out of the blue he said, "The scars that I bear on my soul from ministry are sergeant's stripes in the spirit." I almost fell over. How could he have known what God was talking to me about?

I still feel like an infant in my understanding of how God views suffering, but I can absolutely affirm that it differs greatly from what I initially assumed. God does not delight in our pain, yet he sees an outcome that is more important than our comfort. If he sacrificed his own son for our greater good, what is he asking us to sacrifice in order to help others? It's a question I may be wrestling with for the rest of my life. But I can affirm that I've seen more joy, faith, perspective, and humility in those who have suffered than in those who have not.

LEADERSHIP THAT FORGIVES AND PUTS OTHERS FIRST

After I had completed nine years of reporting across Canada and internationally, David Mainse's daughter-in-law Ann Mainse asked me to help take her show, *Full Circle*, from weekly to daily episodes. I had been a monthly co-host on the show and was thrilled at the opportunity to invest more. I made the difficult decision to leave reporting to help host and launch *Full Circle* daily.

Around this time, new people came into leadership, and the favour I'd always enjoyed in my career disappeared. It was a devastating turn of events for me. As I grieved this, I complained about the seeming injustice of it to those closest to me. But I knew that this response was not what God would want from me. A tug of war began within me. I started to think deeply about the call on my life. If I really believed I was called to be a leader in Canada, then I had to take the Bible seriously and stop making excuses. The Bible tells us in Luke 6:27–28, "love your enemies! Do good to those who hate you. Bless those who curse you. Pray for those who hurt you" (NLT). So I tried to do just that.

Over the course of two years, I committed myself to forgiving those who were hurting me. Through many nights of pain and tears, I prayed for them. I complained and then repented. And repented again. And eventually God showed me that forgiveness isn't just a decision; it is also an action. He opened up opportunities for me to show kindness. I remember having two chances to help someone who had hurt me. Immediately after these opportunities, the person was removed from my life and entered a season of suffering hardship. But amazingly, in my heart I took no joy in it. I only felt compassion. I knew then that God had done a deep work in me. The very next day, I unexpectedly received national recognition for my work. It was if God was saying to me, "You passed the test, and now I will begin to restore you."

I also reflected during this time that the leaders who had profoundly impacted my life were not necessarily those with a title. They were co-workers who knew without words when I was facing hardship and who cared for me and prayed for me. I wanted to emulate their example. I realized I had much to work on to become a godly leader. I needed to learn to put others first, to stop being so task-oriented that I missed the suffering of my co-workers, and to pray for those around me. I didn't need a title or a position. I could lead right where I was planted. But I don't want to make it sound like I was suffering nobly during this time. I wanted out! I updated my demo reel and resume and tried to get a job elsewhere. But nothing opened up.

ALLOWING GOD TO WRITE MY LEADERSHIP STORY

Two years before my season of wrestling with forgiveness, I had a dream about an assault on a school. Someone told me in this dream that God was going to set a table before me in the presence of my enemies, which is a reference to Psalm 23:5. I saw this happen during those difficult years. I not only had the privilege of hosting and producing *Full Circle*, but after it was cancelled I was able to produce stories on behalf of Crossroads Relief and Development all over the world. Finally the door to the travel and justice work I'd dreamed of had opened. I produced stories and helped raise funds for projects in Uganda, Kenya, Ukraine, Tanzania, Haiti, and Puerto Rico. I also was invited to participate on the board of Ratanak International, one of the foremost charities in Cambodia fighting sex trafficking, a cause very close to my heart. I joined 50 women from around the world to climb Mount Kilimanjaro on behalf of sexually trafficked women, which was one of the most amazing experiences of my life. There are more stories to tell than there are pages in this book. God was indeed setting a table of feasting before me in one of the hardest seasons of my life.

I think back now to the girl who was sobbing her heart out at the prospect of travelling to these remote and hard places. I can't even believe it was me. God has brought me to an entirely new place. When I work in the Majority World, I feel impassioned and fulfilled. I have a sense that this is why I'm on the earth. I don't want to glamorize it. The conditions are hard. But the people we are serving live in those conditions. We will leave after a few weeks—they can't. It brings perspective to our brief discomfort. I've had food poisoning in practically every developing nation we've visited, but ultimately it doesn't matter. Along with our partners, we have been able to work to change things. It's an incredible honour. I hope I get to do this work for many years to come. But I'm letting God write the story. Because it's his story, not mine.

Not long after that painful season, doors began to open up for me to co-host *100 Huntley Street* from time to time. I am tremendously grateful for those who saw my potential and gave me opportunities to grow. I'm also thankful for the many hosts who came before me. Former co-hosts such as Moira Brown, Jim Cantelon, John Hull, and Ann Mainse were my mentors and cheerleaders. I can't thank them enough. Eventually, I was given the opportunity to become the full-time co-host and senior executive producer of *100 Huntley Street,* which is how I serve today.

Sometimes it's very easy to watch the public lives of leaders and make assumptions about how they got there. But after doing thousands of interviews and watching how God has worked in my own life, I can assure you that the call to godly leadership is also a call to face hardship. Because of the influence you will wield, God will work to take the rough edges off of your character. You will have tremendous power to both influence and wound, and that power must be stewarded carefully. Leadership is an incredible privilege. It's a call to serve others with your entire heart, to empower and mentor people, and to seek God's direction and wisdom every minute of the day.

As God continues to lay out his vision to me, I've often asked him, "Why me? Why are you opening that door for me?" I know all of the good, bad, and ugly about myself. But he clearly tells me that it's not about me at all. It's not about my worthiness or unworthiness. It's his plan for my life. He's writing the story he wants to write. I'm usually hanging on for the ride! I don't want to miss one minute of the story God is writing for me because I was afraid, unworthy, or unwilling. I wish that for you as well. My best advice to you is to be brave, guard the purity of your heart, hold on to grace with all that is within you, and understand that God will use you despite you, not because of you. You can rest in the truth that his plan is being worked out in your life, as long as you keep saying yes! Live courageously, my friend. I can't wait to see all that he does through you.

Delighting in the Call to Live Loved

Moira Brown

As soon as I could make sentences, I was enthusiastically telling the stories of Jesus that I loved to hear in Sunday school. I was such a defender of truth that my mother thought I might become a lawyer. I did not grow up in a Christ-centred home, but like 60 percent of Canada's population in the late '50s and early '60s, the Hunt family was in church on Sunday. All six children were christened, and other life events were sealed, in the sanctuary of our local church, but none of us found Jesus there.

THE SEEDS OF GOD'S CALL

Evidence of eternity in my heart (Eccles. 3:11) was preserved in home movies. A classic episode shows me—a "tweenager"—with two girlfriends whom I had coaxed to don matching white skorts and red T-shirts for a Christmas pageant—in August! I was the producer of this unusual event on our side patio for an audience of parents and siblings. Mom wouldn't allow us to use my new brother for the part of baby Jesus. We were left with the nemesis of the neighbourhood doing his best to look serene with a brass bowl on his head for a crown, as my friends and I—"We

Three Kings"—proceeded reverently in step with the carol and presented the nine-year-old Ricky with living room ornaments representing gold, frankincense, and myrrh. My desire to please God was partly fuelled by a conviction that there are only two possible destinations after this life. I needed to be sure that heaven would be mine.

Our home was volatile and plagued with drama. Gordon John Hunt, my father, was eight years older than Mom. His father had deserted a wife and six children during the Depression. Love to my dad meant providing for his family. After serving as a paratrooper in WWII, he established a successful cleaning contracting business in Peterborough, Ontario, with his brother Vernon. They later opened an office in Belleville. Dad was a workaholic.

My mother, Margot Louden, came to Canada from Scotland in 1949, at age 18, with her mother and sister. Three older half-siblings had been part of a blended home filled with tension, especially after their father died. Mom had survived scarlet fever and other hardships during the war. Her insecurity showcased a desperate need to be loved and accepted. A history of brokenness and addictions to alcohol and prescription drugs led to many periods away from home for recovery and treatment. Satanic strongholds imprisoned her.

No wonder I plowed through snowdrifts on school snow days to reach my kindergarten class. One day I was the only student there.

Miss Bailey said, "Moira, would you like to take out a puzzle?"

"Okay," I said.

Everything was always okay in Miss Bailey's class. It was safe, colourful, and life-building, with daily Scripture reading and prayer before our snack—in the public school system! Cora E. Bailey had a profound influence in my life. You didn't leave her classroom without a tap on the head—the no longer permitted "meaningful touch"—that said, *You are a person of value and worth; you matter in my world.* Miss Bailey was the first consistent model of God's unconditional love in my life, and on May 6, 1989, at 80, she read the Scriptures about love at my wedding.

When I was 12, I learned the catechism to earn what I thought was my ticket to heaven. With a church membership certificate written in beautiful calligraphy, I thought my business with God was done.

I was no longer attending church when a school friend invited me to a Good News Bible club, where for the first time I learned that I was a sinner and needed to personally receive Jesus Christ as my Saviour. John 3:16 directly addressed my concern. It had me at "not perish but have eternal life."

Unfortunately, I understood the sinner's prayer as an eternal layaway plan: when you die, you meet Jesus, and a wonderful life with him begins! Thankfully, "the LORD looks at the heart" (1 Sam. 16:7). He knew I didn't just want a quick fix but to be right with him. He honoured my earnest prayer to come into my heart just in time for the most painful chapter of my life.

On January 6, 1970, Uncle Vern appeared at the door. There was no reason to suspect trouble, but a mysterious cushion came around me and a clear impression: *something's coming, but it's going to be all right*. Moments later, we were all called to the living room. Mom was weeping. My uncle said, "Your father died today of a heart attack while skiing."

My parents had been separated for three months. Now the stability and anchor of our lives was gone at age 47. Mom, 39, was a widow with six children, aged 6 to 15. Everyone crumbled in shock and disbelief. I felt strangely held up.

In the chaotic weeks and months that followed, I never lost the sense that everything was going to be all right. Years later I solved the mystery: "The eternal God is your refuge, and underneath are the everlasting arms" (Deut. 33:27). God was there all the time.

Oswald Chambers, in *My Utmost for His Highest*, said, "Our soul's history with God is frequently the history of the passing of the hero. Over and over again God has to remove our friends in order to bring himself in their place."[1] The loss of my earthly father ignited a longing for my heavenly Father. In an anthology for English class I wrote, "Whoever may hear: where do I go, and who will steer me? Who will stand over me to say I'm doing right?" I believed there was a best for my life. I didn't want to wing it or blow it. And clearly, I didn't know the One who held my future.

GOD DETERMINES OUR STEPS

I wanted to make people happy. I was seriously considering a career in social work, but in grade 12 my schoolmates elected me to represent them in the

---

1. Oswald Chambers, *My Utmost for His Highest*, July 13 devotional (New York: Dodd, Mead & Co., 1935).

1971 United Way competition—an honour that changed the trajectory of my career. As part of the competition, I had to deliver a speech. I chose to talk about my family's experience with a "little brother," as Dad had been a volunteer and founding president of the local Big Brothers chapter. My speech came from the heart.

The next morning, with the dubious title of "Miss Community Chest," I was interviewed at the local radio station.

"We like your voice. Will you do some more things for us?" they asked.

A new FM station was just being launched. I became a disc jockey, announcer, and music programmer, missing about a third of my final year of high school. I loved playing Frank Sinatra, Percy Faith, and Shirley Bassey—middle-of-the-road music was familiar territory for me, as Mom had filled our home with music (and was obsessive about good grammar and diction). When the program manager announced a raise from $1.60 to $1.70 an hour, I naively thought, "All this and heaven too!" Without question, I over-delivered and was probably being exploited but had no regrets. This was hands-on training for a broadcast career I had not envisioned. There is great truth in Proverbs 16:9: "We can make our plans, but the LORD determines our steps" (NLT).

Two great summers as a radio boat reporter followed at CKLY in Lindsay, Ontario, where I was also off-season receptionist and music director. I'd just started a daily radio show when I was invited to audition for a television co-host position at CKVR in Barrie, Ontario.

The only female TV talk show host I was familiar with was Adrienne Clarkson of *Take Thirty*. "A perfect Ming vase" is how one article referred to the journalist and stateswoman, who would later serve as governor general of Canada. In contrast, I consider myself to be the poster girl for 1 Corinthians 1:27: "God chose the foolish [least likely] things of the world."

My first solo interview was unnerving. I hadn't heard about anything going on with the "youth in Asia" to warrant a 30-minute segment. The press kit introduced me to a new word: "euthanasia." Surprisingly, a few months later CKVR Barrie gave me my own program. At age 20 my continuing education was live on air daily, and sometimes the cameramen doubled over at my bloopers. Having a curious mind and a genuine interest in people, I found it a delight each day to be producing and hosting *The Moira Hunt Show* (1974–81).

My early years of television were the days of close-ups of talking heads against a black background—too intellectual, colourless, and boring for me. I'd been deeply impacted by show and tell in kindergarten and wanted to use television in a similar way—it was a visual medium, after all! For an early episode I asked to showcase a local 56-piece school band.

"We can't light it, and the sound will be awful," I was told.

I pleaded that they just try. If it failed, I wouldn't ask again. Thankfully, my "promote and persuade" approach worked, and so did the show!

What followed for seven years was unending surprise and fun—from Arabian horses in full regalia to a camper van ready to tour the world with two boys fighting and crying inside while I interviewed the parents! The crew enjoyed crafting themed sets. At least once a month we featured a world-class chef in the kitchen. The famous and the obscure visited our Barrie studios. My job was to create a safe, welcoming place, just as I'd experienced in kindergarten, where people could tell their stories. I loved it. I remember thinking, "If I die tomorrow, I can't complain; life has been so good to me."

But questions began to surface in the midst of unimagined blessing. *What about a career move?* CBC's "star maker" had come calling after I guest-hosted a couple of their productions in Toronto. The performance pressure of the big city and the production style of back-to-back tapings didn't appeal to me. I enjoyed spending unhurried time with guests I had chosen, which the "sausage factory" didn't permit. *Was marriage for me?* I knew my boyfriend wasn't husband material. Also troubling was the nuclear threat that loomed large in the mid-70s. *What if someone got to the infamous button and turned the world into a mushroom cloud before morning?* Those thoughts weren't conducive to good sleep. And there was a deeper disquiet … *What if … I died? Would I for sure go to heaven?* I'd compromised my own standards by this time.

Right around the time that these questions were stirring, I read that 3,500 women had gathered in Kitchener-Waterloo for a weekend conference on the Bible with an organization called Women Alive. *These women must have problems*, I concluded. It didn't sound like fun to me.

The founder of Women Alive, Nell Maxwell, lived in Barrie. I called and asked her to be my guest on the program to talk about the issues and concerns of women in the '70s. "But easy on the God stuff. This is not a religious show," I cautioned.

Nell was insightful, and I felt I could trust her. I'd heard that the Bible prophesied the end of the world. She saw my spiritual need, and over lunch in 1978 she responded to my query about God's plan with a compelling bestseller, Hal Lindsey's *The Late Great Planet Earth*. What a comfort it was to see through Scripture that everything God said would happen on this planet had taken place just as he said! Years later, I heard a former chaplain of the US Senate, Dr. Richard C. Halverson, speak at an event. He capsulized the assurance I found: "God is not a victim of history; he is in charge."

I rejoiced that I could finally sleep at night! But the best was yet to come. John 17:3 was a spiritual grenade to my soul: "Now this is eternal life..." What, now? Where? "...that they know you, the only true God, and Jesus Christ, whom you have sent." *Know* him? Know *him*?

I knew *about* him. I'd jumped through every spiritual hoop presented to me, but now the presence of the living Lord Jesus Christ right there in my bedroom was taking my breath away. I knew he wanted my life—*now*! Whatever I had to relinquish was worthwhile to gain the love I'd longed for all my life: "He brought me out into a spacious place; he rescued me because he delighted in me" (Ps. 18:19).

A WHOLE NEW WORLD

Like C. S. Lewis, I was "surprised by joy" and so many other evidences that I was a new creation. One example of my changed heart was how I began to feel about people who mistreated me. One of my superiors at work was a misogynist. He seemed determined to make my life miserable. When I hadn't seen him for several days and was told he was ill, I actually felt compassion for my antagonist. "Jesus really must be living in me," I marvelled, "'cause I know how I feel about that guy!" He became a Christian years later, and we enjoyed happy fellowship together.

My family had drawn closer with Dad's passing, and the Lord liberated me to speak the words "I love you" to my family members and give generous hugs. My siblings were awkward at first but soon eagerly welcomed the embraces. I pleaded, "Lord, if you'll straighten my mother out and make her normal, I'll love her too!" His response was another wonderful book, this time by author Evelyn Christensen, called *Lord, Change Me!* Weeks after I read it, my mother called, saying, "Moira, we're

becoming such good friends. You're less critical and judgmental of me."
Gulp!

The Moira Hunt Show now had a divine executive producer, who was clearly sending guests my way. One of them, though 50 years my senior, became a friend and mentor in my new life. Ruby Henley went to heaven in 1996 at age 97. Bedridden for the last 15 years of her life, she was still dangerous for the Kingdom. "I don't want my life to be all leaves and no fruit," she would say, referring to John 15. Ruby demonstrated Proverbs 13:14: "The teaching of the wise is a fountain of life, turning a person from the snares of death."

For some time, I was a "secret service" Christian, feeling like I didn't belong with the "holy people." I was stunned when a conference speaker sent me off with a heartfelt "God bless you in your ministry!" I didn't have a "ministry" or even qualify for one, I thought.

Soon after, the Lord shifted my perspective permanently, instilling confidence and self-worth that past tiaras and titles never could. The epiphany dawned: I could meet the Queen, because I belong to the King of kings! From then on, my identity has been that of a true princess and daughter of the King with a royal commission as his ambassador and minister of reconciliation (2 Cor. 5:19, 20). This is my favourite word of encouragement when speaking to an audience, and I have often donned a tiara and royal garb to drive it home.

The Lord sent another program guest to direct me into a nurturing church community after I delivered a VHS recording of our interview on the night of their weekly prayer meeting. When a sweet older woman crossed the room to welcome me, the reluctant visitor, the Spirit of the Lord was in her handshake, saying, "You're home!" The family of God was life-building and faith-enriching. The apostle Paul's testimony quickly became mine: "Everything else is worthless when compared with the infinite value of knowing Christ Jesus my Lord" (Phil. 3:8 NLT).

Invitations increased to share my testimony at churches in the wide broadcast area. At one point I wondered if it was the Lord's will that I automatically say yes. His response was clear at a luncheon where the verse at my place was Exodus 33:14: "The LORD replied, 'My Presence will go with you, and I will give you rest.'"

EQUIPPED TO BE AN AMBASSADOR FOR THE KING

The promised rest would come in a fairy-tale setting far from the intensity of my busy life, but not before I had the opportunity to tell many people why I would make the choice to leave an enviable career. Program ratings, salary, and perks had never been better, but I began to feel unsettled in this place of blessing. People were seeing a change in me. Letters from viewers poured out life's trials. When a top chef was preparing a recipe in the kitchen set on a live program, my thoughts were of the people watching. I hoped the half-hour would be a brightener. Perhaps the featured recipe would revolutionize dinnertime, but I knew the One who could transform their lives, and I was talking about fish! At the end of a full year of increasing frustration, prayer, and pleading, the Lord's direction surprised everyone.

"Why don't you go to Capernwray?" my friend Mary Bond said matter-of-factly, referring to the Bible school in Lancashire, England.

Of course! I'd so enjoyed hearing the principal, Billy Strachan, at Fairhavens Bible Conference, where the sign at the entrance made my heart leap: "Sir, we would see Jesus" (John 12:21 KJV). But Bible school in England's Lake District began in four months. I didn't have the airfare, let alone the tuition.

A Holy Land tour that spring with well-known pastors Bill Crump and Bill McRae was a fabulous foundation for the studies to come, but it had eaten up my savings. (The Lord's provision of an emergency flight out of Athens following the 1981 earthquake was an unforgettable demonstration of his protection and preservation at the end of that trip.)

Concerned about the proposed adventure, my spiritual mother Nell said, "Moira, work for a year, save your money, and then go."

Anyone could do that. It didn't require faith or risk. This was an important early lesson in hearing the voice of the Good Shepherd and following his lead. Nell would provide a huge trunk for my venture, and the Lord would send an unlikely benefactor whom he had charged with lending me the money. Church family and friends were supportive too.

FORGING MY OWN PATH

After seven years at CKVR, I felt I should give plenty of notice at work. What a grand surprise send-off I received with two studios full of interview guests and a wall-to-wall gourmet buffet! "Tears, flowers and farewell as Moira leaves the stage" was the local newspaper headline. And how thrilling to later hear that two co-workers, knowing I wasn't crazy, concluded this God must really be something and found Christ for themselves!

Unfortunately, my family was distressed about the transition. One brother said, "Moira, there might have been hope of us coming over to your way of thinking, but now that you're doing something as stupid as this, you've really blown it!" Jesus divides a crowd.

Final packing in Peterborough was challenging because my mother felt sure I was joining a cult. Amidst my packing and Mom's panicking and posturing, Mary Bond gave me a pen engraved with my name and Revelation 3:8. It was the assurance I needed: "I know your deeds. See, I have placed before you an open door that no one can shut. I know that you have little strength, yet you have kept my word and have not denied my name."

People questioned the decision to go so far away with Bible schools closer to home, but the Lord knew I needed to be separated from the pressures of celebrity and a pressing priority of seeing my loved ones saved. It took a long time for God to convince me of Isaiah 43:11–12: "'I, yes I, am the LORD, and there is no other Saviour ... You are witnesses that I am the only God,' says the LORD" (NLT). This vital clarification of roles and responsibilities eventually led me to surrender my family to him.

The most important year of my life, spiritually, began in the fall of 1981. Before school started, I had a profound encounter with the Lord. Early one morning, just as the sun was rising on Morcambe Bay in Lancashire, I reflected on my three-year journey with Christ and all I had been privileged to do *for* him. After this time of equipping, surely I would be a more valued and worthy servant. God silenced that whole line of reasoning. Nothing I had done or ever might do affected the unconditional, unearned love that engulfed me. Jesus loved me, *just because*.

At Capernwray, the Bible was our sole text and rich feast. So many fogs cleared under the teaching of Major Ian Thomas, Dr. Alan Redpath, Stuart and Jill Briscoe, F. F. Bruce, the young newlywed "Torchbearer" Charles Price, and others. I attended a conference for pastors and lay leaders with David Watson, the "Billy Graham of Britain," who shared his ongoing struggle with depression that had been known only to his wife for years. "The secret of successful ministry is the willingness to be vulnerable," Watson said. "We identify with one another not on the point of our strengths, but our weaknesses." These words spoke deeply to me. Transparency has been foundational whenever I speak or lead women's Bible studies.

FAITH NEEDS TO BE TESTED

I didn't realize we were expected to leave the school during holidays. Thankfully, I had relatives in England and Scotland, all of whom needed the Lord. What exciting adventures those trips were! A student rail pass made travel easy and affordable.

For many years I'd corresponded with an aunt in Kirkcaldy, Scotland, and I knew about her love of "the dramatics." On my first visit with her, The Kirk Players were presenting "The Woman and the Soldier," a play about King Herod's Massacre of the Innocents, after which a panel of intellectuals (including my aunt) led a discussion on everything from nuclear disarmament to infanticide.

When a man in the audience bravely suggested that sin was man's root problem, my spiritually resistant relative turned to her minister and said, "I don't think we sin. Do you think we sin?" Pulling thoughtfully on his beard the minister answered, "Well ... we do make mistakes, but I wouldn't say we sin."

My heart started to pound with an urge to tell the truth! But how could I? My aunt would be mortified. The Spirit's prompting intensified until I feared my chest would explode. "Okay, Lord," I said, "I'll stand up, but You had better do the talking!"

The minister answered my raised hand, identifying me as "the visitor from Canada." Romans 3:23 was on my heart: "For all have sinned and fall short of the glory of God." I don't remember what else I said, but it flowed effortlessly.

Stunned silence followed. Then energetic applause! Afterward, the woman who played the lead role came to me with tears in her eyes. My words had reminded her of a Sunday school painting. I knew she was going to say it was Warner Sallman's image of Jesus knocking at a wooden door. I reminded her that in the painting the "door to our heart" had to be opened from the inside, and God reminded me never to be "ashamed of the gospel" (Rom. 1:16). As we left the hall, the minister offered a disclaimer:

"We don't talk about sin here; we leave that to Billy Graham and the like when they come through." My mother's prediction that I would become a vocal defender of truth was sealed in that moment.

Christmas 1981, in the home of relatives in the north of England, was tougher than expected, but it became my most memorable Christmas. With none of the carols and crèches that celebrate Christ's birth, and no close kin, the true gift of Christmas, Emmanuel, was "God with me" as never before.

On Christmas Day, there was a call from Canada. All three phones at home were engaged by a full house of siblings, spouses, friends, and Grandma. Even the dog had a turn to bark!

"Where's Mom?" I finally asked.

There was furious whispering. I heard, "Don't tell Moira." Then came the alarming news. After 11 years of sobriety, my mother was drinking and missing. I had my first and only panic attack. Quietly, I retreated to my room, not wanting to spoil the day for my hosts.

My immediate thought was to get on a plane and head home. Firstborns typically assume the role of caretaker, social worker, and fixer. Reality check—I had no money. Next thought: if I have to sort this out, I might as well go home. What's the point of spending a year learning about a God who isn't big enough and whose Word has no relevance where the rubber hits the road?

Remembering "God's Exchange Program" in Isaiah 61, I prayed, "Lord, will you exchange this spirit of despair, this paralyzing fear, for your joy?" Wondrously, I rose from my knees wrapped in the presence of the Lord. For the rest of the week, with no news from home, I had joy in my days and I slept in heavenly peace. My dear mother called New Year's Day—sane, sober, starting over.

At the end of nine marvellous months, before leaving England, I made a return visit to a little Anglican church in Collyhurst, outside Manchester, where I'd served with fellow students. The pastor and congregation encircled me in the parking lot and laid hands on me, praying that the Lord would use me as an encouragement to Canada. Years later, 1 Timothy 4:14 would remind me of their send-off: "Do not neglect the spiritual gift you received through the prophecy spoken over you when the elders of the church laid their hands on you" (NLT). These beloved brothers and sisters in Christ couldn't have imagined I would have a national platform and be called "television's encourager" any more than I could!

IDEAS THAT TICKLE AND NAG

While at Capernwray, I heard the principal, Billy Strachan, challenge 200 students from 22 countries, representing 19 denominations: "Has God given you a vision? If not, ask him for one!" Not wanting to miss out on anything the Lord might have for me, I did. There was no lightning bolt, just the notion that I would enjoy visiting people in their homes, encouraging them in the things of the Lord over a cup of tea or coffee and perhaps a baked item. That didn't sound very ambitious. Certainly not a viable career option. Yet, in the Bible we are told not to despise the day of small things (Zech. 4:10). I'm reminded of Farmer Hoggett in the movie *Babe*, who learns, "Little ideas that tickle and nag and refuse to go away should never be ignored, for in them lie the seeds of destiny."[2]

Seven years after discounting my vision, I found myself visiting people daily in their homes and encouraging them in the things of the Lord as I interviewed Christians of all ages and backgrounds on the national Christian television program *100 Huntley Street*.

Little ideas that tickle and nag and won't go away may have a great future. I've learned to look for these four characteristics of a vision:

- Simple—you can see it, and your gifting wants to respond to it.
- Impossible—it's bigger than you and outside your comfort zone.
- Strangely persistent—it keeps coming around.
- Not an ego trip—it's about the greater good and God's glory.

But God tells us that "the revelation awaits an appointed time" (Hab. 2:3). When I graduated from Capernwray, it wasn't yet time for my vision to be fulfilled. I left England having no plan but absolutely certain that God did! It was surprising, and a little disappointing, when CKVR TV reached out, inviting me to return to host a daily program. It was too bizarre that the only one-bedroom apartment I could find available for rent in Barrie was the one I had left! Was I returning to "same old" after all?

---

2. *Babe*, DVD, directed by Chris Noonan (Los Angeles: Universal Pictures, 1995).

Suddenly, both doors closed. The Lord wanted me to understand that there is nothing I can sacrifice for him that he can't restore. There is no place for pride in following him. He is no one's debtor! Billy Strachan was right in saying, "Your ministry will begin in the place where they know the worst about you." I went right back to CHEX TV in my hometown, writing commercials and co-hosting *HOSANNA,* a weekly Christian program on FM.

I held a Bible study for co-workers in my mother's home, where I'd landed, and found great joy taking God's Word to a seniors' home each week. For three months I moved across the street to live with a precious widow, Mrs. Calendar, after she had a stroke and rapidly advancing dementia compromised her safety. What a thrill it was to lead this lifetime churchgoer into a personal relationship with Jesus!

One of my brothers called me "Mission Moira." Romans 15:7 in *The Message* expresses our calling: "So reach out and welcome one another to God's glory. Jesus did it; now you do it!" My focus was on people who needed the Lord, and I felt responsible to respond to every need that crossed my path. After all, don't we have all eternity to enjoy God's family?

A dear friend came for a weekend visit and pleaded, "For once, can I be one of your needy people?" Galatians 6:10 was a wake-up call: "Therefore, whenever we have the opportunity, we should do good to everyone—especially to those in the family of faith" (NLT). In a letter my friend spoke "the truth in love" (Eph. 4:15), expressing concern that the enemy had me so busy running after many things that I might be missing God's plan and purpose. What a comfort to read God's promise in Psalm 32:8: "I will guide you along the best pathway for your life" (NLT). Recalling all he had invested in me, I quickly realized that a need doesn't constitute a call. I began to seek "his good, pleasing and perfect will" (Rom. 12:2).

Dr. Terry Winter brought his evangelistic crusade to Peterborough—the Canadian city with the most churches per capita in 1985. I couldn't organize my purse, but he asked me to be office manager, leading to many enjoyable months of interdenominational teamwork for the Kingdom. That same year, I participated in a Toronto Christian women's conference. The keynote speaker attended my workshop. Dr. Jean Barsness, Canada's first female missiologist, approached me afterwards and said, "We need you at Briercrest Bible College!"

Now in my early 30s, heading to the wheat fields of Saskatchewan for Bible college didn't make sense. A letter of invitation arrived from Briercrest's Media Services Department. I didn't respond. There seemed to be an irritating number of Saskatchewan licence plates on the highways that summer. Weeks of turmoil ensued, but Job 22:21 was right: "Submit to God, and you will have peace; then things will go well for you" (NLT).

I surrendered to God's plan and enrolled at Briercrest. While assisting with media production and classes, I was happy to be studying God's Word again in the fall of '85 and gaining a critical understanding of belief systems that were permeating the culture.

A Lone Ranger mentality had fuelled my zeal for the Lord and the lost, but my solo flight crashed in the wheat fields of Saskatchewan. Shanghai flu, immediately followed by pneumonia, sentenced me to bed for weeks. I'll never forget the comforting hug of two slices of buttered toast delivered with love by a single faculty member. I couldn't even read—my eyes hurt so much.

As I listened to Scripture on tape, the Holy Spirit personalized Jeremiah 30:21: "'I will bring [her] near and [she] will come close to me, for who is [she] who will devote [herself] to be close to me?' declares the LORD." I couldn't return to Ontario until I had produced all the summer *Briercrest Bible Hour* programs and sent them out to radio stations. The Lord made his priority clear: "Being always precedes doing!"

During the summer of '87 I visited the huge St. Lawrence Market in Toronto and was utterly amazed at the sea of consumers. How many, I wondered, were strolling thoughtlessly into an eternity separated from God? I had the strongest urge to get on the public address system and make an appeal to the captive crowd. I also found myself that summer on a 50-foot boat, cruising Georgian Bay with special guests David Mainse, president of Crossroads Christian Communications, and his entire family. He made me promise that if I was recruiting for Briercrest again the next summer, I would give my testimony on *100 Huntley Street*.

When I graduated from Briercrest in 1988, every door seemed closed. It was frustrating to know that other students had neatly organized plans for the summer. I felt trapped in the wheat fields. The Holy Spirit highlighted a most unusual encouragement, Psalm 113:8: "he seats them with princes, with the princes of his people." A chapel speaker's closing challenge gripped me: "If you're ready, you won't have to get ready." I was uncomfortably aware of the extra 20 pounds I was carrying!

Dr. Paul Magnus, then vice-president of Briercrest, graciously invited me to pursue graduate studies. But first, I returned to Ontario, where I appeared with Nell Maxwell on *100 Huntley Street,* as promised, to tell how our meeting led to my salvation.

One week later, I was called out of my first grad studies class for a long-distance call from Toronto asking me to pray about becoming the first full-time female co-host of Canada's longest running daily television talk show. Wise summer lecturers helped me process this unexpected opportunity in weeks of essential teaching, and a loving Caronport community in the prairie I'd grown to love caught the vision.

"Go with God!" was on the farewell cake. When the glowing candles caught fire, Evelyn Budd, wife of President Henry Budd, said it was prophetic, but more than Holy Spirit fire was waiting. A fiery *trial* was on my horizon!

FACING MY FEARS

Years before, I had said, "God, send me to Africa, but don't ever ask me to live, work, or drive in Toronto!" But after accepting my new job, I could say along with Job, "What I feared has come upon me; what I dreaded has happened to me" (Job 3:25).

After my uncle co-signed a loan for a reliable car, I tackled the first treacherous trip into the big city. As I descended into underground parking, an angelic chorus on the radio was singing, "We are climbing higher and higher." The Lord seemed to be enjoying an "I told you so!" moment as I drove home on the nerve-racking Gardiner Expressway, accompanied by "The Triumphal March" from Verdi's opera *Aida!* Jesus said, "with God all things are possible" (Matt. 19:26). If he brings you to it, he will bring you *through* it!

I quickly discovered that Crossroads' vice-president of finance and administration lived just two blocks from the apartment where I was staying with my youngest brother in Mississauga. Many mornings it was my joy to be Richard Brown's passenger for the long drive. I had assumed he was married when he interviewed me for the position. Contentedly single, I didn't give it a thought.

The family I returned to was distracting, however. Drugs, alcohol, and reckless living were threatening to steal their physical lives before they could be rescued spiritually. For 10 years I'd been praying for their salvation, but God didn't seem to be doing anything. I proposed a desperate measure—telling the Lord he could take me home. Consumed with guilt, remembering all my passionate appeals, my loved ones would surely capitulate and come to Christ at my funeral. Proverbs 19:2 was a key lesson: "Desire without knowledge is not good—how much more will hasty feet miss the way!"

The Lord seemed to appreciate my enthusiasm and willingness to sacrifice, but he gently pointed out that my family didn't need another funeral.

"How about a wedding?" was the shocking alternative!

I realized that growing up no one in my family had even one example of a Christ-centred home or marriage. God was calling me to provide that model. Soon after this scary proposition, I wakened in the night, wrapped in ... a wedding veil! (The white sheers in the window behind my bed had blown over the headboard.)

BETTER TOGETHER

God is a romantic! I could write a book about his wooing me out of singleness weeks before the so-called "most eligible bachelor in Canada" asked me for a date. Co-workers conspired to encourage the match. Soon my heart was singing a tune from *My Fair Lady:* "All at once am I several stories high, knowing I'm on the street where you live!"[3]

Richard asked what I wanted for my birthday in March. "A handsome prince" was my reply. A six-week courtship and seven-week engagement led to "I dos" before hundreds in St. Paul's Church in downtown Toronto on May 6, 1989. The hour-long ceremony was later televised to the nation on *100 Huntley Street*.

I had harboured a concern that marriage would diminish my potential for the Lord. The restorative power of the love of Christ through Richard brought healing I didn't know I needed, and our diverse gifts and strengths have enhanced our efforts and increased our joy for three decades.

---

3. Vic Damone, "On the Street Where You Live," Columbia Records, 1956.

MOTHERS ARE LEADERS

My first pregnancy miscarried in 1990—a grief I'm thankful to understand. The next year our precious daughter Katherine was born. Five months later my mother died suddenly at 60, the same year she surrendered to Christ and was wondrously transformed, finding the peace she had sought all her life.

Through all these life events I was prayerfully supported, celebrated, and richly comforted by God's family. I've kept countless cards and letters from faithful viewers and taken great delight in responding with handwritten correspondence.

Davy arrived in 1993, 17 months after his sister, and the Lord began to tug at my heart and sanity. I was a mother of "a certain age"—39, to be specific! A bookmark from my friend Jane Magnus was defining: "Slowly, softly, quietly may you grow to accept the changes in your life with courage." None of those adjectives fit the wind tunnel I was living in. Our home was a landing strip! Isaiah 40:11 reminded me that God "gently leads those that have young." In this high-demand season as a working mother, I ceased to enjoy the things that had given me joy—typical of burnout.

A sympathetic woman in a coffee shop shared her struggle with work/life balance: "I was always juggling and constantly on edge," she said. That was me! Co-hosting the weekly *Just for Parents* TV show with producer Bruce Stacey provided sage advice for what my husband calls "the greatest adventure." One author on the show delivered a knockout blow: "Yes, we are making memories with our children, but more significantly, *I am the memory*."

I thought about Miss Bailey and how she influenced my childhood, though I couldn't remember much of what she did. *Who we are* to one another is of more ultimate value than *what we do* for one another.

I noticed that whenever we were going anywhere, Katherine would say, "Mommy, we have to hurry before it closes!" To my horror, I realized that I was cultivating panic in the heart of a preschooler! Henry Ward Beecher was right when he said, "The mother's heart is the child's schoolroom." I began to think more about how my priorities were affecting my children. A viewer sent a song on cassette about the demands of offices and telephones, pleading, "but who will lead the children to Your throne?" The lyrics cut deep.

My pathetic petunias provided a potent parable of this pooped parent! Their blooms in early spring were so big and bountiful that my neighbour, an expert gardener, asked where I had purchased them. By mid-summer, the showpiece pink blooms were puny pale struggling bugles at the end of spindly elongated lime green stems, too far away from their source of nourishment.

"Have you fertilized them?" my neighbour asked.

"Uh, no ..."

"You need to cut them back."

My conservative snips didn't satisfy the eyes of experience that watched as I reduced the stems to stubble (and removed the unsightly pots from view). Two weeks later, I witnessed a miracle. The petunias were restored to their former glory! God was giving me a portrait of the pruning that would rescue me. *Finding Focus in A Whirlwind World* by Jean Fleming framed this chapter in my story:

> Busyness that is not God-directed and God-motivated is not God-blessed. Busyness can ravage the soul as thoroughly as idleness can. We may live in an illusory world remembering greener days, without recognizing that our zeal has waned. But if we keep busy enough the truth can't penetrate and expose our spiritual condition. Our visible external life may be laudable, but our inner spiritual life has shriveled.[4]

Jesus warned, "You cannot be fruitful unless you remain in me ... for apart from me you can do nothing" (John 15:4–5 NLT). My heavenly Father's patience and sense of humour was abundant in getting me to level ground. I considered the option of staying at home with my children. I was never good at math, but the idea of leaving thousands who need the Lord for two little people didn't add up. Luke 12:48 had long been my conviction: "When someone has been given much, much will be required in return; and when someone has been entrusted with much, even more will be required" (NLT).

The wrestling match ended September 1993 at Disney World in Florida, where my favourite ride, Dumbo the Flying Elephant, was boarded up. The sign in bold letters said, "DUMBO IS TEMPORARILY CLOSED FOR

---

4. Jean Fleming, *Finding Focus in a Whirlwind World* (Dallas: Roper Press, 1991), 56–57.

RESTORATION. HE WILL FLY EVEN HIGHER WHEN HE REOPENS SOON." I knew who Dumbo was! I resigned from two boards, said "no" to every speaking request for a year, and in April 1994 took a seven-page handwritten letter to David Mainse explaining how the Lord was leading me to stay at home.

GOD REWARDS OBEDIENCE

On my first day away from *100 Huntley Street*, I wasn't at home either, because Hollywood actor Tim Allen had taken up residence there. The Disney movie *The Santa Clause* seized our townhouse for five-and-a-half weeks of filming, which required us to move down the street to an empty condo that backed onto Lake Ontario. How important to be with my little ones in this strange new place (and the financial blessing was right on time!). The cable guy connected us to Family Channel, and the first show to appear was *Dumbo's Flying Circus*!

Home*making*, I would quickly learn, is a literal word. I needed to rediscover my need of the Saviour, be restored in my first love (Rev. 2:4), and invest in his most precious gifts—my husband and my children—in that order. My sweet spouse had been taking up the slack.

A word to the wives: motherhood can be all-consuming, and the "squeaky wheel gets the grease," but we are not "one" with our children (Gen. 2:24). My own parents' tragic marriage highlighted the missing key in Ephesians 5:33: "each man must love his wife as he loves himself, and the wife must respect her husband" (NLT). I also discovered it's impossible to love your neighbour if you're never home.

En route to New Brunswick to a final speaking commitment, I read Mary Farrar's book *Choices*. She said not to fear putting your career on the back burner to make parenting a priority. How right she was! The next 12 years went by so quickly. At about the halfway mark, my eyes filled with tears of gratitude for this growing season in my life when I saw a small plaque in a card store that said, "She is happiest, be she queen or peasant, who finds peace in her own home" (Goethe). Years later, my 24-year-old son Davy would spend many hours viewing and editing home movies to present me with a heart-melting reminder of what I might have missed.

CHARACTER IS DEVELOPED THROUGH TRIALS

After my husband's 10 years with Crossroads, the Lord had an unexpected redirection for his career path too, one that would stretch him as never before. Together, we would learn the truth of A. W. Tozer's words when he said, "It is doubtful whether God can bless a man greatly until He has hurt him deeply."[5]

Three and a half years of underemployment was no walk in the park, but the Lord had Richard right where he wanted him—on his lap and in his Word early every morning. From Genesis to Revelation, "the poor and the needy" seemed to rise from the pages. Richard also sought the Lord's direction in many excellent books. Chuck Swindoll's *The Mystery of God's Will* was illuminating:

> Our human tendency is to focus solely on our calling—on where we should go, how we should get there, and what exactly we should do about it. God's concern is the process that He is taking us through to mature us and ready us, making us more like His Son. In other words, all of us—including you—are works in process.[6]

God used Richard's season of underemployment to restore his lost dream of working with the poor in Africa. Years earlier, Richard had hoped to become a medical missionary, only to face disappointment and betrayal when he didn't get into med school. The Lord used a host of head hunters and dashed hopes of leadership positions with mission organizations to rekindle the call he had planted long before.

On December 3, 2010, after three hours of verbal ping-pong in our living room—Scriptures and insights focused on the suffering and marginalized, the widow, and the orphan—our friend Jim Cantelon asked Richard to pray about working with him. There was no hesitation in the response: "I've been praying for three and a half years. This is it!" We were willing to go overseas, but Jim asked Richard to establish a ministry office in Burlington. The Crossroads Centre would provide a base five minutes from our new home.

A month later, in Africa, the chip on Richard's shoulder over the Lord letting him down began to dissolve with many tears of repentance and

---

5. A. W. Tozer, *The Root of the Righteous* (Camp Hill: Christian Publications, 1986), 137.
6. Chuck Swindoll, *The Mystery of God's Will* (Nashville: Word Publishing, 1999), ix.

gratitude. Richard began to travel several times a year to Africa as the international director of Working with Orphans and Widows (WOW), and we made two trips to Africa as a family. The Lord's leading to homeschool the children in 2004 would facilitate a five-and-a-half week excursion to Malawi, Zambia, and South Africa. The following year our international team of 12 spent Christmas in Zambia, celebrating with gifts and meals for hundreds of children. We witnessed how the work "caused the widows' hearts to sing for joy" (Job 29:13 NLT).

Richard's experience of wrestling with his calling taught us an important leadership lesson: leaders must learn to wait on God's timing to align with his purpose. The authors of *Experiencing God* beautifully express this principle:

> When God is ready for you to take a new step or direction, it will be in agreement with what He has already been doing in your life. Sometimes, you may find yourself in difficult or confusing circumstances. To understand these events, God's perspective is vital.[7]

A NEW PURPOSE FOR A NEW SEASON

While Richard was spending time overseas and our children were spreading wings of independence, I was riding the emotional roller coaster produced by the unhinged hormones of menopause, and I felt not needed.

Through tears, sitting in church alone one Sunday in the fall of 2005, I wrote a poem to the Lord: "Is it heaven, or meaningful purpose I'm longing for?" I wondered. Two days later, Ann Mainse called from Crossroads asking if I would join the "Sofa Sisters" for a new weekly women's TV program called *Full Circle*, launching in January 2006. God's surprises were just beginning.

On October 3, 2006, I returned to the interview set of *100 Huntley Street*. It was the anniversary of my first day as program host in 1988. The guests were graduates of Teen Challenge Farm, where a judge had permitted my brother Ian to enrol instead of going to jail. Ian died in 2005 at 47, but the Lord interrupted my grief with a profound peace that came with affirming words—"All is well."

---

7. Henry Blackaby, Richard Blackaby, and Claude King, *Experiencing God: Knowing and Doing the Will of God* (Nashville: B&H Publishing Group, 2008), 196.

The Lord had already demonstrated his faithfulness when my only sister, Kathy, died tragically on May 26, 2002, at 45 due to cirrhosis of the liver. With just two and a half conscious hours left on this earth, after being so angry at God, the mother of two teenagers surrendered her heart to Jesus. The peace she experienced was palpable in her hospital room when 30 people prayed with my husband to release Kath to her heavenly home.

A parade of ministers, missionaries, authors, and mentors joined me in my "sweet spot" back on the *Huntley* set, giving me the privilege of showcasing their spiritual journeys and thanking them personally for helping to shape mine.

In May 2014, two months after my 60th birthday was celebrated with fanfare on air, my first book was published: *Hugs From Heaven: God's Embrace in the Adventure of Faith*, featuring highlights of God's faithfulness and life lessons in all the seasons and circumstances of my life—with colour pictures! Five thousand were printed and purchased. I'm still hoping to refresh and reprint it.

BEARING WITNESS TO GOD'S FAITHFULNESS

Many changes at Crossroads created a climate of uncertainty. In the discomfort, I discovered that C. S. Lewis's words are trustworthy indeed: "God whispers in our pleasure ... but shouts in our pain."[8] Malachi 4:2 was a heaven-sent affirmation: "But for you who fear my name, the sun of righteousness will rise with healing in his wings. And you will go free, leaping with joy like calves let out to pasture" (NLT). Although I experienced God's presence intimately during this time, it was difficult to be released from a job I loved in July 2015. It was a privilege, however, to immediately be asked back to do occasional interviews, keeping that connection with the precious viewers.

Within a few weeks of my release, I was contacted by Joy Radio, asking me to consider a variety of involvements in Christian radio and podcasts—which didn't sound like freedom. What worked was a two-minute devotional airing several times daily on radio. *Hugs From Heaven* was then posted to Faith Strong Today.

Jill Briscoe once told me that the gifts and the spirit don't age. Indeed, Romans 11:29 attests, "for God's gifts and his call can never be withdrawn"

---

8. C. S. Lewis, *The Problem with Pain* (Toronto: HarperCollins, 1940, 1996, 2009), 91.

(NLT). If I could go back in time and give my younger self some advice, I would tell her to live her life with eternity in view! And *never* doubt the goodness of God! This world is the exercise room. The best is being prepared and yet to come, so don't waste time over regret, remorse, or resentments. Keep your heart pure, free from any root of bitterness, so God's best can continue to unfold for and through you. He redeems suffering and repurposes pain. Amazingly, he even orchestrates "do-overs" and "make goods"—second chances. Wait for it!

The enemy of our soul is a tempter. He wants to distract and derail us, keeping us from abundant living and finishing well. When I feel disquieted within, I immediately ask, "What is it, Lord?" The Spirit of truth is usually quick to pinpoint the source of discomfort and a way to restore his peace. When making big decisions, I also use a helpful filter that is posted to my fridge:

1. Can I ask God to bless it?
2. Will it bring him glory?
3. Will it cause someone else to stumble?

Alan Redpath used to say, "Christians need to be RFA—ready for anything." My prayer for the days ahead is "Lord, help me to eliminate and concentrate!" I want to be ready for whatever he has planned next! As the psalmist said, "Many, LORD my God, are the wonders you have done, the things you planned for us ... were I to speak and tell of your deeds, they would be too many to declare" (Ps. 40:5).

Accepting the Call to Learn and Lead

Leila Springer

Growing up in a small village on an island in the Caribbean, I never imagined myself becoming the leader of one of the most prestigious breast cancer organizations in the world. The very idea of leadership seemed so far removed from the reality of my early years that it was almost absurd.

I grew up on the small island of Barbados. It is perhaps the most beautiful of the Leeward Islands with its breathtaking landscape and pristine shores. Our little island in the sun is bordered by the Caribbean Sea on the west and the Atlantic Ocean on the east. I lived on the north end of the island, where the air is fresh. Depending on how close you are to the coast, you can sometimes smell the ocean breeze as the wind off the Atlantic blows across the fields on the north shores. It is easy for the people of Barbados, located below sea level, to sometimes feel a bit isolated. When you look at the string of islands on the world map, Barbados is situated off on its own, escaping the wrath of the many deadly Caribbean storms and hurricanes and faced only with strong winds and rain.

Growing up, my friends and I never gave much thought to our geographical location. As children, we had other things to occupy our young minds and keep our little world exciting. We were free to be ourselves and wander around the community, knowing that we were cared for by all of the adults in sight. This was truly a time when the village raised the children and bore responsibility for them, ensuring they were well taken care of and kept safe. Spending my childhood in the country was fun, and I hardly ever ventured to town until it was time to attend high school.

Elementary school was within walking distance of our home, and it was there that I learned many of life's lessons. The motto of our school was "thoroughness, punctuality, regularity and obedience." This four-legged stool would form the basis of my character and follow me throughout my life.

Church was the centre of my family's life. We went to church on Sunday mornings and to Sunday school in the evenings. We had Bible class on Mondays after school and "young people meeting" (as we called it) on Tuesday nights. These were great times. During my summer holidays, I joined my closest friends—Alvean, Vilma, and Doriel—and some of the younger boys in the neighbourhood to "play church." Many of us didn't have toys, so we used our imaginations to pass the time. We had a "pastor" and a "song leader" (as we called them back then), and we gave testimonies of our life experiences, which were few, but I believe they helped us to deal with our issues by learning early on to take them to the Lord. Each day, our "church" would last from 9:30 to 11:00 a.m. Then we were scheduled to go our separate ways as we brought lunch to our parents, who mostly worked in the fields. Upon our return, we would have church again until it was time for us to prepare the evening meals before our parents came home.

My mother worked in the fields. I remember taking lunch to her and watching the plantation owner on his horse with an umbrella to shade himself from the sun while the women and men worked hard in the fields under the hot midday sun, labouring for the small pittance they would receive at the end of the week for the work they had done. I watched as the women and men hoed the fields or tied the sugar cane, often being told that they were going too slow and needed to be faster. I thought to myself, "I will never do this; I will never work in the fields, being driven like an animal; this is too hard and human beings should not have to work under these conditions."

My mother worked in the fields until she was moved or promoted to working in the plantation house as a helper. At night she would come home and always complain of how she was treated. She would lean on her hand on the corner of our little table and say, "It won't always be like this." I didn't realize it then, but she was saying "this too shall pass"—and it did.

My dad worked in a similar situation, driving a great Caterpillar machine that harrowed the land, preparing it for planting. He always had his own transportation—beginning with a bicycle, then a motorcycle, and finally, a car. My dad was always ambitious but, you could say, lacked opportunity. I remember we were the first ones in the district to ever have electricity. My dad got a bulb, wired a generator, and put the bulb up on a pole to give us light. We were so excited, and all of the children in the neighbourhood came to see our new phenomenon. I thought my dad was a genius. He could do anything, and I knew that he loved me. I was his special little girl.

Daddy's dream was to own a taxi business. While he was working the Caterpillar machine, he kept saying to his children, "One day I won't have to do this; one day I will have my own taxi business and I will be fine." That day did come, thanks to determination and a lot of hard work. Dad began to realize his dream by finding old cars and fixing them himself. I think that is how he got his first car. First, there was an old Ford model, then a Citroen, a Vauxhall, and finally, two Mercedes vehicles—a Mercedes van and a Mercedes car. Dad used both to run his taxi service, because he believed that cars should pay for themselves.

By the time Dad had fulfilled his dream of owning a taxi business, all of his children had grown up and moved away—two of us to Canada and my sister to the US. Dad had instilled in us the value of hard work and the importance of keeping your dream alive, no matter what that dream was. This was a great lesson for me to learn in leadership: when you believe in something, when you feel the passion and speak it into the atmosphere, God hears and will grant your petition, as he did for my dad.

This was my childhood; these were my formative years; this is what I remember as a child, and I loved it. I would not trade anything for my childhood. I believe every experience we have in life is part of our journey, part of our story, and an important part of who we are and who we can become. God, who knows the beginning from the end, was a part of my life, my existence, and continues to be that.

HEARING GOD'S CALL TO LEADERSHIP

God is our unseen agent who uses his wisdom to chart the course our lives should take as we are directed into our respective roles in the tapestry of life. For me, the wind of change began to blow very early, beginning in the corridors and classrooms of the private high school I was privileged to attend. Tuition cost my dad an enormous amount of money, but he saw the potential in me and made the sacrifice so that I could get a good education. God groomed me in the classroom, on the playing field, and through my interactions with schoolmates. All of these experiences were designed to prune and shape me to grow into the beautiful tree of hope that I would eventually become.

I can still remember as a young child being called ugly. I was criticized for my voice, the way I spoke, and the way I walked and looked. As a result of this criticism, I entertained certain beliefs about who I was that caused me to question my true identity, form destructive thoughts about myself, and struggle with low self-esteem. Consequently, I did not have many friends. This continued until the Lord healed me and set me free.

Early in high school, I began to notice certain reactions from teachers that puzzled me. I was asked either to stand in the corner for the entire class, to do all the reading for the class, or to leave the classroom. I could never understand why this was happening and sometimes sat in defiance to the teacher's order because I didn't think I had done anything wrong or that I was worthy of the punishment. I remember being asked to apologize to a teacher, but I wasn't told why, so I refused and was sent away from the classroom. I eventually wrote the note of apology that was requested and made it sound as good as I could. I wrote many things that I didn't mean, but they sounded convincing, so I was allowed to return to the class. I learned an important lesson that day: if you are going to punish someone, at least have the courtesy to tell them why they are being punished and then give them the opportunity to make adjustments.

In spite of these unfortunate incidences, high school was a lot of fun—both in and out of the classroom. Due to the enormous amount of reading I was asked to do during class, my oratory skills began to take shape, making way for the leadership role I would assume later on in life. Reading helped me with my diction, pronunciation, poise, and vocabulary.

Building strong relationships with my school peers came naturally for me. I was always the one in the group everyone looked up to, respected, and approached for help when there was a problem. Without realizing it, I stood out as a group leader at home and at school. Whenever I speak at a board meeting, at church, or in the marketplace, I am reminded of these early years when I was described as the strong one, speaking with authority and commanding attention without effort. I was short, so I guess God had to give me a loud voice to compensate for my lack of height!

I was 17 years old when I heard the voice of God telling me that he had work for me to do. By this time, I was a single mother with the responsibility of raising my first child at a time when I still needed the care of my own mother. So much had changed after I became pregnant at age 16. Some of my friends had rejected me because they did not think it was a good idea to be hanging out with someone who had obviously made a bad decision; someone who was now, in their eyes, a failure. To them, I was clearly not a child anymore. This early experience of rejection helped me to relate to women in similar situations much later in my journey. Willian Shakespeare is quoted as saying, "The choices we make dictate the life we lead," and this certainly rings true for me because I had to live with the consequences of my own decisions.

As I was sitting in the backyard of my village home, thinking of what would now become of me—a young unwed mother—in the stillness of the moment, an unmistakable voice spoke. I couldn't tell where it came from; I just knew that it spoke, and when that voice spoke, I could do nothing else but listen. It was not an audible voice; rather it was a strong inner conviction that I could not ignore. I knew that this was not an ordinary experience. I knew that a voice from the distance was beckoning me to join him in building his Kingdom and leading others to follow the path of righteousness. But at the time, I hardly knew how to pray, nor did I understand the power of prayer and the marvellous things that could be accomplished through prayer.

Although I gave my life to Christ and accepted him as my Lord and Saviour, I soon made some more unhealthy decisions that drove me away from God. For the next 12 years, I wandered in the wilderness of fear, low self-esteem, and insecurity that gripped me so tightly that I couldn't seem to shake myself free. Then finally one day, my Master saw me helpless and stretched out his arm to me once again. This time, I took his hand, and my journey of leadership began to take shape.

RESPONDING TO JESUS

"God is calling you. Today if you hear his voice, harden not your heart." These were the words I heard in my dream; a man had stood beside my bed and uttered these words. I knew these words were from the Bible, but I didn't know where to find them. I decided not to tell anyone about the dream—I thought it was too spooky. However, after having that dream, I kept recalling my childhood Sunday school lessons and the hymns I had learned at school.

Deep down in my heart, I knew change was on the horizon, but I tried to ignore the signs. By this time I was 18 years old, trying to find employment after completing my business studies and taking care of my young son. I had just gotten engaged to Alvin, my son's father, whom I had met while in high school. Alvin had left to make a new home in Canada with hopes for us to join him after he was settled. After joining Alvin in Canada 13 months later, I became quite rebellious towards my faith. I wanted nothing to do with church; I tried to convince myself that God was not real, and if he was, he certainly did not care for me. Life had become very hard, trying to settle down and find a job, so I blamed my problems on God.

When Dad came to visit me, I told him I wanted nothing to do with the God he served. I told him that if there was a God, he had to be white, because life was good for white people but black people always seemed to struggle. My dad listened in shock and then told me that he knew I didn't believe what I was saying. He said I would come back to the God I pretended not to believe in after my season of questioning. He wondered why I was praying every time I had a problem and singing so many hymns and worship choruses. He couldn't understand how I had become so religious but still didn't go to church.

It was New Year's Eve 1979, and Alvin and I did what we always did as a young couple—we went out dancing and had what I thought was a marvellous time. I danced all night long and went home at 3:30 in the morning. In a few days it would be Sunday. I finished the year on the dance floor with no thought of what I would do with the rest of my life, but the dreams of God calling me kept coming back to my mind. I knew I needed to make a change.

I began the decade of the seventies with Alvin leaving me to migrate to Canada. Now, at the beginning of the eighties, my heart was beginning to soften towards God. My life would not be the same as previous years, although I didn't have a clear plan of how anything would change. I just knew that those dreams were in my head and I could not ignore them. God was calling, and I needed to respond. He would not keep knocking and waiting forever.

I tried several churches but couldn't find one that made me feel at home. Finally, I decided to try the Seventh Day Adventist Church. I reasoned that the Adventists must be right since they worship on Saturdays and the Bible talks about honouring the Sabbath. I looked in the Yellow Pages directory and found an Adventist church that was not too far from where I lived. "OK, good!" I thought. "That's where I am going on Saturday." I made plans for the week to make sure my work was all done by Thursday so that I could start my Sabbath on Friday; however, on Thursday a lady came knocking at my door. I believe she was directed to me so that I could begin my new life in Christ.

I had just finished my work and was relaxing on the sofa when the doorbell rang. I went to the door to find a lady (who lived down the street) trying to sell me some Avon products. To this day I don't know what made me invite her in, but before I could think it through, we were talking about Avon cosmetics in my living room.

Somewhere in that conversation, I happened to say to her, "Do you know a good church where I can attend? I am looking for a church to attend with my children."

The woman repeated: "You are looking for a church?"

I said, "Yes."

She responded, "Then why don't you come with me on Sunday? I go to Agincourt Pentecostal Church at Birchmount and Huntingwood. If you are ready at 10:30, you can come with me."

I didn't need any more encouragement! I could hardly wait for the days to go by so that I could go to church on Sunday. I got up early and prepared breakfast for my two boys, and we got dressed. We drove down the street to meet the lady, and off we went to church.

Church was beautiful; I loved it. I joined in the singing and will never forget the words to the song that touched my heart:

Jesus! What a friend for sinners!
Jesus! Lover of my soul;
Friends may fail me, foes assail me,
He, my Saviour, makes me whole.
(J. Wilbur Chapman, "Jesus! What a Friend for Sinners!" [1910])

After listening to the choir and the sermon, I heard the altar call for those who wanted to accept the Lord Jesus Christ as their Lord and Saviour. This was my moment to make that final decision, but I was a bit shy, so I waited for the first person to move, and then I followed. With my head bowed and tears streaming down my face, I stood at that altar with a counsellor beside me. She put her arms lovingly around me and helped me say the sinner's prayer and rededicate my life to Christ. I had done what Dad said I would do. I came back to the God I pretended not to believe in.

Proverbs 22:6 says, "Train up a child in the way he should go: and when he is old, he will not depart from it" (KJV). In my case, the child would not wander too far from her roots. After rededicating my life to Christ, I was home, and it felt good. Three months later, I was baptized and started on my new journey with the Lord.

SPIRITUAL PREPARATION FOR LEADERSHIP

I joined the New Life class at church and was encouraged to read my Bible every day and pray regularly. I loved my class; it was small, and everyone was friendly. Each week it seemed like forever for Sunday to come around again. I desperately wanted to learn all I could about God, and I knew in order to do that, I had to be involved in church meetings outside of the regular Sunday morning services. I went to church on Sunday nights, Wednesday nights, and any other night there was a meeting. I devoured everything I could put my hands on that talked about God and his love for us.

One Wednesday night, I came home from church and felt what I now know to be a strong sense of the Holy Spirit. I rushed through the doors after parking my car, ran upstairs to my room, knelt beside my bed, and poured out my heart to God. I opened up the Bible and read the following passage from Isaiah 55:12–13:

"For you shall go out with joy, And be led out with peace; The mountains and the hills Shall break forth into singing before you, And all the trees of the field shall clap their hands. Instead of the thorn shall come up the cypress tree, And instead of the brier shall come up the myrtle tree; And it shall be to the LORD for a name, For an everlasting sign that shall not be cut off." (NKJV)

I wasn't sure what it meant except that I was called to lead and had the promise of God to help me along the way. I closed my Bible. A few days later, I got another Scripture:

"Son of man, I am sending you to the children of Israel, to a rebellious nation that has rebelled against Me; they and their fathers have transgressed against Me to this very day. For they are impudent and stubborn children. I am sending you to them, and you shall say to them, 'Thus says the Lord GOD.' As for them, whether they hear or whether they refuse—for they are a rebellious house—yet they will know that a prophet has been among them." (Ezek. 2:3–5 NKJV)

After reading this passage, I knew that my ministry would be developed and that it would have a focus on people of African heritage; these were my people. I just didn't know how, when, or where. I wondered how my ministry would be to people of African heritage if I was in a predominantly white church. It didn't make any sense, but I was humble enough to wait for the answer from God, which would come 20 years later. In leadership, when God asks you to do something, it will not always make sense, but all we are required to do is trust him. Allow him to guide you in the path of righteousness as you serve where he plants you.

I felt strongly that I should attend Bible school but couldn't imagine how on earth that was going to happen while my children were very young and I didn't have the money. I asked God how he could ask me to go to Bible college when he knew it was impossible practically and financially.

But then one Sunday in church, the pastor announced, "I know many of you would like to go to Bible college but can't afford it for many reasons, so we are going to bring the Bible college to you." The church arranged for teachers to be brought in from Eastern Pentecostal Bible College to teach any willing students. I was the first to sign up and there began my formal studies in the Word of God. I would later attend Canada Christian College before transferring to Tyndale College, where I enrolled in religious education courses.

I later joined a small prayer group that met every Saturday night in various homes. I was soon afforded the opportunity to become a member of my church's steering committee and began learning the importance of moving in the Spirit and understanding the hand of God on your own personal life as well as on the lives of the people you are called to lead. Getting to know and being led by the Holy Spirit was something I practised but did not quite understand. I spoke to my pastor about my concerns, and he encouraged me to get involved in an area of the church and allow God to do the rest. He assured me that becoming busy for God is the best way to learn his voice and follow in his footsteps. This was good advice for a person like me who knew so little but understood that there was much more to learn as I moved through my spiritual journey.

That small prayer meeting gave me the opportunity to see myself first and then the people I was called to serve. I began to see areas where I needed to be refined, chiseled, and shaped into the very image of Christ. Where I was overly aggressive and brash, God slowly began to change me so that I could become pliable in his hands. As prayer group members began to comment positively on my devotional messages, I thought back to my unfair treatment in high school. How grateful I am that I didn't allow early discouragement to sway me from speaking publicly! Still, I did not see the positive feedback as a call to lead. I was doing what I enjoyed and loved: sharing godly wisdom from the Scripture with others. My prayer was always that I would please God. If I ever got the opportunity to speak to anyone, I prayed that I would only share words of wisdom and substance. God answered my prayer.

People were hungry for the Word of God and had a strong desire to draw closer to the Lord. Several people in the group gave leadership by being part of the steering committee. Leading a group of 75 to 100 people with very little experience can be challenging; nevertheless, we took on the task and trusted God to lead us. I was barely in the group before I began to realize the impact I was making. There were phone calls and requests for prayer for various needs. There were questions about the Bible as well as requests to explain various Scriptures. I began to feel the pressure of not being good enough to answer questions. My lack of knowledge led me to delve deeper into the Word of God. It also forced me to read more, beginning with my Bible and then widening my choices to acclaimed spiritual writers, like F. B. Myers and G. Campbell Morgan, whom I came to love and respect. I attended additional Bible classes and conferences and sat at the feet of great scholars. All this was in preparation for the position I would hold later in life, but at the time, I was so busy learning that I was not totally aware of what was transpiring in terms of these new spiritual leadership roles.

Good leadership comes by learning the lessons that life hands you. God led me from being bullied and feeling the need to be always on the defensive to learning how to overcome fear and rejection, embracing the promises of God, and trusting God to lead me into his truth. The greatest example I have had along the way has been that of our Lord Jesus Christ. He knew why he came to earth. He declared, "For this cause I was born, and for this cause I have come into the world" (John 18:37 NKJV).

There is no greater leader than Jesus. He set out to meet the needs of people, beginning with his disciples, whom he taught how to live and how to lead. People who followed Jesus did not fully understand who he was but always knew that his words were fresh and pregnant with meaning. Through his teaching, their lives were transformed.

I began to believe that if I followed the example of Jesus and continued the path of becoming more like him, I would be all right. There are some things we learn in school, others we read in books, and other lessons that are gleaned from great pastors, preachers, and teachers. However, I believe more is gained from our own personal experiences, by falling down, getting back up, understanding our vocational calling, and persistently following guidance from the Holy Spirit. Gaining spiritual guidance means developing a closer relationship with God and following in his footsteps as you move forward to do what he has called you to do, regardless of what that might be. Learn to hear his voice above all the other voices that seek to distract us.

NEW BEGINNINGS AND NEW STRUGGLES

Walking this spiritual journey with the Master can be interesting. Following in his footsteps does not always give us the advantage of seeing what is ahead; we must trust him one step at a time.

Around this time, I moved to a new church, where I began to teach Sunday school. As Easter approached, I felt the need to work on a short skit with the children about the story of Easter. Little did I know that this endeavour would open the door to a new chapter as I allowed God to lead me.

My first Easter skit soon became a huge drama presentation with live animals and a full set. It was exciting. The church, which seated over 1,500, was jam-packed the first night. I was shaking in my boots, wondering to myself if this was really happening. The accuser of the brethren never ceases to take advantage of our fears, and soon I was hearing questions in my head: "Who do you think you are? Do you really think you can put on a production that people will enjoy, and do you think someone might actually come to know Christ through the story?"

As the questions swirled in my head, I felt a sensation like a surge of whirlwind, and the presence of the Lord enveloped me as my heart opened up to allow the Holy Spirit to minister to me. The reassurance of his call to me for ministry was renewed as his words of comfort, courage, and peace filled my soul. He spoke in love, reminding me that the production was not about me but all about him, and if I would only trust him, everything would turn out just right.

The first production was a huge success, and I would go on to write and produce several more productions for my church, drawing an audience from as far away as Buffalo. I marvelled as people drove miles to see the Word of God demonstrated by Christians who were gifted in a unique way to share the gospel of Jesus Christ.

———————————

The hands of time gradually changed again, this time on a more serious note. I was about to walk through an experience that would eventually lead me to a higher calling. In the middle of practising for the Easter play in 1999, I was diagnosed with breast cancer. My whole life was threatened, my soul was battered, and my strength was failing. My only hope was in God, and I leaned heavily on him for the strength and courage I needed for the journey I was now on.

In hindsight, I can see how God used this painful season to shape me into the leader he needed for the ministry he had called me to. He knew that working with women who had contracted a critical illness such as breast cancer would take someone with special qualities of love and compassion. I was not sure I had either of these at the time, but a period of recuperation gave me time to be in much prayer, to read, and to commune with God at a higher and deeper level than I was used to. This new commitment would be my road to developing a heart and love for women who were vulnerable after a diagnosis. I had to endure hardships and pain in order to develop the qualities I needed to serve effectively.

There is no substitute for time spent reading the Word, praying, and preparing your heart before God for the direction needed to lead his people. Reading gives us the knowledge we need to deliver the message of hope. I often refer to a quote I heard in a sermon preached by George Jeffrey Williamson. He used the story of an old preacher from the South who was once asked how he became such an effective preacher. The answer was unique—and in broken English—but quite powerful. He said, "First, I read myself full, then I pray myself hot, and then I let go." This has been my mantra: to read as much as I can, pray as Paul directed us to—without ceasing—and then stand with godly confidence and lead God's people to victory.

LIGHTING A FIRE OF HOPE

The diagnosis of breast cancer took me through a period of darkness that I call my "dark night of the soul." At first, I was preparing to die, and then I bargained with God. I told him that I could not ask him to keep me alive and live as I did in the past. I told God that if he would show me some new things and teach me some new lessons, then I would continue to serve him passionately until he called me home.

One day after a bout with chemotherapy, at a time when I was at my lowest, I cried out to God from the depths of my spirit, not for myself but on behalf of other women who might be experiencing similar pain and anguish as a result of cancer treatment. I recalled my experience in the pharmacy when I went to collect my oral medication after my first chemotherapy treatment and almost fell over in shock at the cost of it. But my concern quickly turned to those less fortunate who had to struggle to make ends meet and to take care of their families while enduring the hardship of cancer treatment.

While I thought on these things, God asked me to start something that would benefit women who were receiving cancer treatment but did not have anyone to support them, especially during the days when family members and friends were at work. God uses the hardships of life to light a fire of hope in our hearts. He can take what the enemy meant for evil and use it for our spiritual good. God used my hardship to plant the seeds for a new ministry—the Olive Branch of Hope. I didn't know how this ministry would begin or unfold, but I sensed his call to start a support group for Christian women with breast cancer.

One lesson that stands out to me from this season of life draws from Numbers 8:4: "This is how the lampstand was made: It was made of hammered gold—from its base to its blossoms. The lampstand was made exactly like the pattern the LORD had shown Moses." God knew that the purpose of the lampstand in the tabernacle was to give light. The people of Israel had come through the wilderness after a period of darkness, hardship, and intense thirst, but they were on God's journey to the Promised Land. The lampstand was to give light in the tabernacle and was not to be covered; therefore, it was put through a process and hammered out according to the pattern of God's instructions. I believe that in leadership we are called to shed light in this dark world, and sometimes we too have to be hammered out in order that God's perfect pattern and design can be seen for his glory.

Part of my hammering was a diagnosis of breast cancer. If I hadn't walked through that valley, I would not have been equipped to understand the trauma one endures from the treatment, the emotional roller coaster ride one is subjected to, or the mental stress and uncertainty that accompanies survivors throughout their lives, even after treatment. A diagnosis of cancer often causes people to question their faith in God, wondering if they are being punished for not obeying him. But, in the stillness when we look up, the words of Romans 8:28 can be our comfort: "all things work together for good [our spiritual good] to them that love God, to them who are the called according to his purpose" (KJV). The key here is a distinct call. We must know that we are called to do the work we are engaged in.

ACCEPTING THE CALL TO LEAD

How I became the president of the World Conference on Breast Cancer Foundation (WCBCF) was nothing short of a miracle. A fellow breast cancer advocate (whom I had met at a breast cancer conference in Halifax, Nova Scotia) encouraged me to apply for a seat on the board of WCBCF. I quickly declined, but my friend continued to encourage me. I never contacted WCBCF to discuss the possibilities of serving on their board; strangely enough, they contacted our office to see if anyone would be interested in joining the board in representation of the black community.

I was on the WCBCF board for barely one year when things began to change. After serving on the multicultural committee, I was encouraged to accept a role as one of the executives. I settled for vice-president and was comfortable with that position until I received a call from Barbara Shumeley, who was finishing off her term as president and wanted me to consider stepping in as her replacement. At first, I said no. Surely there was someone else who would step up. I encouraged the board to keep searching and hoped that by the time I got back from my trip to Barbados, it would all be settled. However, I returned to find out that the board was waiting for me to get back before they made the final decision.

I accepted the role as president with much fear and trepidation. My appointment to lead at another level was clearly in view, and I felt a surge of fear of the enormity of the task, but God never left me alone. He was there to face every challenge with me. When I did not know what to do, he gave me the answers. When people were not responding to my requests for meetings to help organize the conference and I was feeling discouraged, he showed me the answer.

One morning, I awoke feeling deeply discouraged, and I contemplated giving up. I just could not understand why I felt like I was being ignored and shoved aside by the establishment that I needed to partner with if the organization was to be successful. What was the reason for their total disregard for my many requests for meetings? I had no answer for the reason, until one day I opened up my computer and, lo and behold, an email that was not meant for my eyes was in my mailbox, containing the answer: I was the first black president of WCBCF and was not expected to succeed.

While some encouraged me to make the discovery public, I responded, "I don't believe that's why God revealed this truth to me." I believed God wanted me to know the reason for the problem I was facing. He had called me to new heights but not without challenges. However, I knew he would see me through to the end. I received a long letter of apology from the person who made the derogatory statement, and I accepted it. The board accepted my reason for not pursuing this problem further, and I was happy they did. I trusted God, and he came through for me. My success did not depend on man but on God. When he calls, he equips, and he leads the way, and we follow.

The call to lead as president of the World Conference on Breast Cancer Foundation gave me the opportunity to meet people from around the globe and see the needs of women first-hand. Indeed, it was a blessing. I served on the board for two years and then three more as president. At the end of my term, I passed on the leadership to someone else with the knowledge that God wanted me to give my undivided attention to my first assignment, the Olive Branch of Hope. Today, I still work with women all around the globe and I still communicate with those I met through my work with WCBCF. Sadly, some have passed on, but those who are still alive are as much a blessing to me as I am to them.

As for the World Conference on Breast Cancer Foundation, I learned that the board at the time was having problems finding a new leader. They asked me to consider another term, which I declined. Leading such an organization at that time was quite stressful and challenging. After much discussion, the board decided that the organization had run its course and decided to dissolve it in 2012. Although I was sad at this decision, I felt good that I had left the organization in good financial standing with a cushion of $400,000. The funds were distributed to like-minded organizations, and I was rather surprised to receive a cheque for $37,000 for the Olive Branch of Hope.

THE OLIVE BRANCH OF HOPE

My first responsibility was to my people, meaning people of African ancestry. This was what I was called to do according to the Scripture I was given: "For you are not sent to a people of unfamiliar speech and of hard language, but to the house of Israel, not to many people of unfamiliar speech and of hard language, whose words you cannot understand" (Ezek. 3:5–6 NKJV). I knew I needed to stay focused on my mission as commanded by God. With the help of fellow breast cancer survivor Winsome Johnson, whom I met at church, I gathered the courage to ask six others to launch a cancer support group. This wasn't an easy task due to the code of silence that exists in our community.

Eventually, the Olive Branch of Hope was born. The ministry grew and began to provide support groups, educational seminars, and faith-based support for women of African ancestry diagnosed with breast cancer as well as breast cancer survivors who want to learn more about the disease in order to support others. Presently, we serve women in the GTA, including Peel Region, Markham, Durham, and Hamilton. We also get calls from others outside this catchment area.

Our team learned that women of African-Caribbean heritage are often diagnosed with cancer at a much younger age than other ethnicities and are often faced with a more aggressive form of the disease. We heard stories of women on various islands who were being diagnosed too late and dying before the age of 45. This prompted us to extend our reach to underserved developing countries in Africa and the Caribbean, especially in the rural areas where most of the problem lies. We conduct seminars and workshops annually and give vouchers to cover the cost of mammograms to encourage women to get tested early.

I can still remember attending a networking event with one of our researchers from McMaster University, Dr. Juliet Daniel, who was sharing some information about her findings regarding black women and triple negative breast cancer—a strain of the disease that affects women of African ancestry disproportionately. It occurs at an early age, is very aggressive, and can sometimes be fatal. Dr. Daniel shared her latest discovery, indicating that the aggressiveness of the cancer was first thought to be due to late diagnosis and lower socio-economic status of this ethnicity. Her findings added to those previous findings but also revealed a possible genetic cause. This was good information for us to know and helps us as we continue to carry out our mission.

At the networking event, the then CEO of the YWCA walked up to me after the session and said, "Congratulations, Leila!" I looked at her, somewhat shocked at her comment. She continued, "This all happened under your watch, under your leadership. This is fantastic work that you are doing. Keep up the good work." Until then, I had not given it much thought. I was doing what I thoroughly enjoyed—helping others—and not expecting any accolades, but I looked back at her and simply said, "Thank you." I had answered the call of God, and it led me in a path I would never have dreamt of—an unusual path, but one that still allows me to serve. For this I received several awards, including an Award of Excellence from WCBCF and a Woman of Resilience Award from Women's Health in Women's Hands.

THE POWER OF INFLUENCE

In February 2015 I attended an event in downtown Toronto where the special guest was the then candidate for prime minister Justin Trudeau. I had the opportunity to take a photograph with him, which I proudly posted on my Facebook page. Needless to say, the photo received many "likes" and positive comments from far and wide, which I embraced, beaming with pride. However, there was one comment that did not go on my public page—it was sent through Messenger and gave a strong rebuke for taking a picture with Mr. Trudeau. The woman who wrote the message was quite annoyed that I, a Christian, would take a photo with Mr. Trudeau, knowing that his values did not quite align with Christian beliefs and faith. She noted that as a woman of influence in my community, I should be more careful of my associations and the message I was sending. Without giving it much thought, I fired back a response that I have lived to regret to this day.

The lesson I learned from that experience is one that I should have known, but in a moment of weakness and unpreparedness, I was caught in the wind of the enemy. God would use that experience to ground me and remind me that leadership is also a position of influence; therefore, many people are affected by my words and actions. Clearly, I must pay close attention to my responses to situations that confront me in this role of leadership.

You are not a leader if no one is following you, and no one will follow you if you don't influence them with your lifestyle, knowledge, wisdom, and intelligence. In order to lead by influence, it becomes necessary to build strong relationships with those you are called to lead. We follow the example of Jesus, who called himself the Good Shepherd, and we are his sheep. Jesus is our influencer, and we look up to him for guidance and strength as we work with others.

LEADING BEYOND THE BORDERS OF CANADA

I know that God chose me for a position of leadership that goes beyond the borders of Canada. This became plain after I was asked to be president of the World Conference on Breast Cancer Foundation. I understood then that I would lead not only by influence but through strong relationships, though building them would be a challenge. After all, working with different cultures around the globe can be very difficult.

I quickly learned that people who share the same skin tone can be very diverse and have many cultural differences; understanding and celebrating them is key to forming strong relationships. Working with women in Zambia, Tanzania, Uganda, Kenya, and, of course, the Caribbean became a school of learning. The diversity among the diaspora is enormous, but so it was with the children of Israel. David ruled first over Judah and then Israel; I can only imagine what challenges he faced as he developed relationships and led with godly wisdom.

The Bible tells us in Romans 11:29 that the gifts and call of God are irrevocable. We make mistakes and sometimes find ourselves out of God's will but are ever-thankful that we are never out of his care. We may choose, like Jonah, to travel to another city rather than obey, but the call of God remains relentless: he hunts us down and allows circumstances to overcome us and eventually push us toward his call. God calls and equips us to fill a vacancy in the Kingdom so that we can help to make this world a better place. So whether from the pulpit or in the field, all are important to God and should also be important to us. We move through the maze of life always knowing that we are not alone and that one day he will reward us for what we have done. Being faithful to the call is our best response.

Living in Unwavering Faith

Marie Miller

When God calls us into his service and shows us his plans and purposes for our lives, we must embrace the call into his wonderful arena with certainty. Each step we take adds a new dimension to our life and will ultimately cause us to become more resilient in all situations. As a female pastor, I have encountered opposition to my calling, but experience has taught me that a key factor in accomplishing and fulfilling my God-given purpose is to learn how to overcome offences. A wisdom chapter in the Bible says it this way: "A person's wisdom yields patience; it is to one's glory to overlook an offence" (Prov. 19:11).

In light of this passage, I encourage you, my sisters, to reach your unlimited potential by understanding your past, practising unwavering faith, and embracing unchangeable examples. Be unbending in the call, be understanding of process, be unashamed of your calling, be unaffected by others' misconception, be open to dealing with unresolved feelings, be unhindered by your femininity, be unrestricted by your status—be an unimaginably mighty woman of God!

UNDERSTANDING THE PAST

My parents, although raised in completely different spiritual denominations, met and married while attending Bible college in Jamaica. Four years later, I was conceived as the third of four children. When I was 12 years old, our family experienced a thrilling yet overwhelming day when we were informed that we would be relocating to Canada. Although it was meaningless to us children at the time, my parents had been in the active process of immigrating for almost five years.

On November 8, 1974, my family arrived in Montreal, Quebec, and our lives embarked into completely new dimensions from that time on. The excitement of moving to Montreal overshadowed the pain of losing all things familiar in Jamaica. My siblings and I enjoyed our first snowfall that November, playing in the snow with exuberance. However, by the next year, my parents had to take us on a visit to Jamaica, as we longed for the wonderful warm climate and for the many familiar things that we now missed dearly.

My father was a man who did not permit excuses, including sickness, to keep the family from church. He had pastored in Jamaica and began serving as a lay pastor at the Church of God of Prophecy in Montreal. In both places, family life encompassed only one thing—church! However, shortly after our relocation, my father announced that he would no longer be involved as a lay pastor with the church, but he adamantly declared that all of his children must attend church somewhere every Sunday. The family immediately experienced diverse deviations to the normal Sunday routine. My mother returned to the Salvation Army, the denomination she was born into and part of until she met my father. My older sister, for a season, continued to attend the Church of God of Prophecy, choosing to remain with her friends. I attended Evangel Pentecostal Church, a Pentecostal Assemblies of Canada (PAOC) church near our home. My older brother preferred not to attend church, and my youngest sister went with whoever left the house first on a Sunday morning.

Meanwhile, my father lost his desire to pastor again and ultimately lost his dream. Being a very private person, he kept all his pain to himself. He died at the age of 88, yet never shared his disappointments, internal struggles, or pain with anyone—except with the Lord, to whom he prayed, both night and day. In the non-spiritual yet profound words of a great female leader, former Liberian president Ellen Sirleaf, "We should never lose sight of what we are hoping for, for our dreams have the size of freedom."[9]

My father initially carried the spiritual temperature and tenacity of our family. A by-product of his new lack of concern for spiritual matters—an unfortunate part of my early developmental years—was that no one recognized the gifts of God upon my life. While I always felt a compulsion to express myself in church, I did not have the luxury of receiving spiritual training within a family setting. There were times when I had a keen awareness of things that I knew were of God, or I would have a premonition, dream, or vision about something. However, those became my own personal inner stories. Some of these instances of spiritual awareness were so vividly experienced that I often thought they were real for others as well. It took almost two decades before I learned that God had given me these intuitive abilities as a gift upon my life.

EMBRACE UNCHANGEABLE EXAMPLES

As a young adult member of my church in the '80s, I was passionate about seeing young adults become serious about their walk with the Lord. For that reason, I belaboured and lobbied the pastoral staff for the creation of a vibrant young adults ministry at the church's annual congregational meeting. Not only did the church approve the idea, but they then entrusted me with bringing the group to fruition. The ministry began with eight young ladies and grew within a few years to a vibrant group of 75 active young adult men and women. I consider this ministry experience the first step in my call as an evangelist. Consequently, the need to have a pastor on staff for this group was finally acknowledged, and to this day, Evangel Pentecostal Church in Montreal has enjoyed decades of vibrant young adult ministries.

However, despite the success during that season, some labelled me as a militant woman or a feminist who felt she could do everything. In contrast, the same gifts that caused me to be labelled as a trouble-maker in the church were praised in my secular working environment. My colleagues took note of my natural leadership skills and considered me a person to watch for future advancement in the company. Nevertheless,

9. Ellen J. Sirleaf, *This Child Will Be Great: Memoir of a Remarkable Life by Africa's First Woman President* (New York: Harper Collins, 2009), 254–255.

I took courage from women who did not fear the odds or become faint-hearted because of the labels placed on them.

The Bible overflows with examples of women who were used as workers for God, in both authoritative and submissive positions. Every person has equality in the mission of God, the mission of leading people to the Saviour. The story of the woman at the well (John 4) demonstrates God's ability to meet people of all walks of life and use them to minister his gospel, regardless of who they are.

BE UNBENDING IN YOUR CALL

Before God called me to full-time ministry, I was gifted as a runner and trained passionately in the 400-metre race, hoping to make the Olympic team. I learned the discipline of hard work and had the ability to endure long, sleepless nights of body fatigue yet awaken the next day to run a race with fervour and an expectation to win. My journey towards the 1984 Olympics, however, ended in a quick loss during the Canadian national trials.

It wasn't long before God turned my discouragement into excitement with an incredible promotion to a position at the corporate office of Canada's national airline, Air Canada. I had been working at Air Canada in the word processing department but was eager to transfer into the marketing department when a position opened. Working with the analysts in the international strategy group became my new career.

Behind the scenes, God was using my new job to prepare me to run a completely different kind of race. He began to weave the pieces of my life together, preparing me for future divine purposes. Having the ability to travel the world with Air Canada opened my eyes to the needs of impoverished countries. In 1988, as I travelled with an Air Canada co-worker to India, I had no indication that my life would change within 24 hours.

Upon arrival in Mumbai, the overwhelming sights, sounds, and smells for which India is known profoundly struck me; however, the overwhelming disparity between opulence and poverty grabbed my spirit even more. In my upbringing and travels, I had never encountered such a contrast. Growing up in a middle-class Jamaican family, I had been sheltered from areas of severe poverty. But here, exiting the Bombay (now Mumbai) airport, I was struck with the shocking reality of what dire poverty looks like.

The stench of the city, the masses of people, and the cries of the beggars in the street became overwhelming to me. My heart broke to see so many children in the streets begging; some even had arms that had been mangled to render them better beggars. Such disparity between opulence and poverty refocused me on the compassion that Matthew 9:36 speaks of: "When he [Jesus] saw the crowds, he had compassion on them, because they were harassed and helpless, like sheep without a shepherd."

Poverty challenged my faith, pulled on the core strings of my emotions, and tore my heart apart. Didn't God create enough wealth in the world for all people to enjoy some of its benefits? My resolve was that this question can only be answered when we make the choice to sacrificially use what God has given us to bless others. I returned home, resigned from Air Canada within a year, and began my journey towards ministry, with a focus on the mission field in my heart.

After resigning from corporate life, I enrolled at Zion Bible College (now Northpoint Bible College) in the US. This experience proved quite shocking for me, a mature student and world traveller who was known for having a strong personality.

In the early '90s, many women attended Bible colleges to become a pastor's helpmate. However, ministry was the only thing on my mind, so this mindset proved difficult to understand. Also, at this same time, my prophetic gifting was becoming operational again, and the Bible college experience presented some unforeseen challenges. One would have expected prophetic gifts to be welcomed in a Bible college setting, but unfortunately that was not the case at first.

On one occasion, I gave a prophetic message in a chapel service about some areas that were grievous to the Lord and gave a warning against such behaviour. The situation was actually occurring while I spoke in a warning tone against it; however, while I was accused of using prior knowledge and wrapping it in a prophetic word, I honestly had no human knowledge of it. From then on, I ensured never to give a prophetic message or share any words of knowledge to anyone. Instead, I buried myself in prayer, and after much deliberation, I transferred to Eastern Pentecostal Bible College (now Master's College and Seminary) in Ontario, where I ensured that my gift remained dormant.

Eleven years after I exited Zion, dissuaded from giving prophetic declarations, to my surprise the new president of Zion requested an audience with me and gave a special appeal asking that I return, by invitation, to preach at the college. Later on, I found out this was done for two reasons:

1. to authenticate the Word of the Lord that had come through this vessel years prior;
2. to restore me so that I would not lose courage in using the gifts of the Lord upon my life.

In moments such as these, you recognize how much God is the Lord of reversal. As I stood up to preach at Zion, the dean of students, Dr. Jo Scruggs, my former professor, introduced me to the school as a woman of God being used in the prophetic realm and a woman called by God for our times. With such a humbling introduction, ministering the Word was made easy and was received with incredible receptivity by both students and faculty. After that day of restoration, I was invited to preach regularly at Zion.

What I still love and admire most about Zion Bible College (Northpoint) is its legacy of powerful women in ministry, its consistent acceptance of women, and the resolute egalitarian position in its DNA, a major factor of its ongoing impact. Although many churches did not make appropriate allowances for women in leadership levels beyond children's ministries, Zion continuously graduated women who were resilient against that Pentecostal grain and were able to find ministries suitable to their gifting.

As I prepared for ministry, I looked for examples of such women in ministry who were unbending in their call. When my journey in full-time ministry in the PAOC began in 1992, I noted that the PAOC had only given very minimal significance or recognition in public to the mighty women in this denomination's ministry. There were very few mentors to glean from, and so searching the history of the PAOC was my only recourse to obtain some format of encouragement. The Pentecostal Assemblies of Canada's archives has records of many remarkable women leaders in the PAOC spanning its entire history. These women include Sophie Nygaard, Marion Keller, Mabel Cunningham, Iris Scheel, Sadie McLeod, and Bernice Gerrard, to name a few. However, not much was written about them, a great disservice to their sacrificial lives and powerful ministries. One of the PAOC's archivists who assisted me in my research, Rev. Jim Craig, calls some of these women the "dynamic duos, i.e., single women who worked together in ministry such as Maude Ellis with Janet Rogers, and Ella Birdsell with Ida Mason."[10] All of these women contributed to the great denomination that the PAOC has become.

My research showed me that many female ministers who came before me shared the same frustrations that I experienced. In the words of Phoebe Palmer regarding the frustration of women whose gifts were hidden by men: "The church in many ways is a potter's field, where the gifts of woman, like so many strangers, are buried. How long, O Lord, how long before man will roll away the stone that we may see a resurrection?"[11]

It is meaningful to note that some of the challenges experienced by Canadian women ministers became more prevalent in the industrialized decade. However, the good news is that leaders in the twenty-first century seemingly noticed this discrepancy, and in the last decade great changes have been made for the betterment of women in ministry. For instance, in 2010, I was voted by the PAOC fellowship of pastors to sit as a member on the PAOC general executive board for two years. Unfortunately, for myself personally, as a single woman, certain conditions have worsened due to societal stigmas and perceptions. Sadly, being confident in one's personhood and gifting is still seen as insufficient if you are not accompanied by a validating spouse.

BE PATIENT WHILE WAITING FOR OPPORTUNITIES

Immediately upon my graduating from Eastern Pentecostal Bible College, Agincourt Pentecostal Church brought me on as full-time staff. This large multicultural church in Scarborough, Ontario, is renowned in the denomination for its size, missional heart, and strong staff. My position was to oversee prayer ministries, cell groups, and singles' ministries.

The egalitarian senior pastor at the time, Rev. Stuart Mulligan, was known and loved by all because of his unique pastoral style. He released all his pastors and staff to develop their gifts amongst the congregation.

10. Jim Craig, interview by author via email, March 16, 2016, the Pentecostal Assemblies of Canada Archives, Mississauga.
11. Phoebe Palmer, *Promise of the Father* (1859), chapter 16.

Pastor Mulligan was a phenomenal preacher who always left his hearers with a spiritual nugget, most often in a hilariously memorable message. Needless to say, with a pastoral staff of 11, having opportunities to preach in the Sunday services proved difficult.

On one of the occasions when I had the opportunity to preach, a reporter from a secular newspaper unexpectedly attended the service and chose to do a favourable write-up on my message. Both the favour of having the opportunity to preach God's Word and then the blessing of God's timing in sending a reporter on that specific day became a marvellous set-up for future ministry progress, specifically when my ministry as an evangelist commenced and required affirmations from a broad arena.

Pastor Mulligan had no problems with women preaching and remained very firm in defending his two women staffers to all who opposed. As far as he was concerned, the person with the ability to command the Word before the congregation would be given the opportunity. His actions lived out Paul's words in 1 Corinthians 11:8–9 in that he did not leave room for either sex to despise the other: "Women can't be interdependent from men because woman was created for man. But neither can men adopt an attitude for prideful disdain for women, since woman was created because of man's need for her."[12]

PRACTICE UNWAVERING FAITH

The journey from corporate lifestyle to Bible college and then into ministry in the church has been a very colourful mosaic. The challenges of meeting and working with people who do not believe that women should be ministers has been quite exasperating. Nevertheless, I've responded to God's call with fervency and without apology, and I've focused on his mission for my life, whatever the cost. I have personally and audibly heard God speak to me, clearly saying that I have been set apart (Gal. 1:15). This clarion call has kept me focused for many years when I was very tempted to give up and walk away from ministry. The resounding inner voice empowered me to practice dwelling in unwavering faith, even in seasons where doubt tried to destroy me.

---

12. Loren Cunningham and David Joel Hamilton, *Why Not Women? A Fresh Look at Scripture on Women in Missions, Ministry, and Leadership*, ed. Janice Rogers (Seattle: YWAM Publishing, 2000), 171.

I believe God has set me apart for his divine purposes. God has, with certainty, called me to the ministry of his Word in the church and in the world. He has equipped me to preach and publicly declare his Word with power and authority. He has gifted me to serve as a leader and evangelist for the purpose of encouraging and lifting up marginalized people around the world to show them Christ. God has gifted me to help others recognize that his power can work in and through the most unlikely people. He has made me a woman with all his creative uniqueness and then anointed me as he continues to prove his call upon my life for leadership in ministry. Isaiah 61:1–3 represents my life verse: "The Spirit of the Sovereign LORD is on me, because the LORD has anointed me to proclaim good news to the poor." God has magnificently proven this Scripture to me throughout many years of ministry.

Over the years of serving in ministry as a single person, I have had to practice unwavering faith when mocked, despised, or overlooked. I've had to maintain extreme discipline in order to travel, often alone, to now 53 countries. At times I've had difficulty pushing through my vision to tend to the marginalized people of the world, both in spiritual and in physical matters, because I speak in a woman's voice into the ears of male leaders. Holding on to unwavering faith remains critical to doing what God has called me to do, even when treated poorly by men who operate within a similar call. Remaining committed to the call and cause of Christ has proven challenging because of constant suppression by male leaders, for over two and a half decades. Despite these challenges, I have had to continue demonstrating an unwavering and relentless faith and adding to that faith, love.

God has set me apart to be an example to people from other cultures and groups, especially marginalized women and singles. I remain thankful that he uses me to minister to all believers, demonstrating to both men and women alike his wonderful call upon a woman's life. God has especially used me in countries where men dominate the lives of women, leaving them without a voice. He has equipped and anointed me to boldly minister and break through stereotypes. I have seen many male leaders change their opinion about women in ministry after experiencing the impact of partnering with women for the sake of propagating the gospel to the ends of the earth.

BE UNASHAMED OF YOUR CALLING

In 1994, my senior pastor presented me with the opportunity to go to Uganda, Africa, to assist our missionaries there by preaching in crusade services. These missionaries were given prime property in the central part of the town of Jinja, and they wanted to host outdoor crusades to draw a crowd in order to begin a church afterwards. Lovingly, my pastor had informed me, "Since I cannot give you my pulpit more frequently, go to Uganda and preach out a lot of the messages in your spirit."

I went to Uganda quite nervously, having never before visited Africa and not knowing what to expect as a woman pastor preaching in outdoor crusades. Later on, that experience provided the first step of my journey towards ministering as an international evangelist. In that town of Jinja, where no Pentecostal church existed prior to the crusade, a large PAOC church was birthed, which has since spawned many other churches. The issue of a woman preacher did not hinder the work that needed to be accomplished. The incredible receptivity removed all fear of my calling and also all the inner embarrassment I would feel at times, being a female leader in male-dominant ministry settings.

BE UNAFFECTED BY OTHERS' MISCONCEPTIONS

After a few years in ministry, I travelled to several other countries and continued to encounter opposition from some male-dominant circles. In these settings, I learned to exercise the words that my mother, Mavis Miller, embedded in my spirit from a very young age: "Marie, bloom wherever you are planted." I must confess: I thrived in doing just that.

Many churches, both in poorer countries and in North America, readily allowed women to lead if the churches were struggling to survive. But if a woman managed to build the church into a thriving congregation, she worked herself out of a job and was generally replaced by a permanent male pastor.[13]

Bible Way Church in Montreal, Quebec, had gone through a terrible split in the congregation, and no other minister wanted to assume its

---

13. Stanley J. Grenz and Denise M. Kjensbo, *Women in the Church: A Biblical Theology of Women in Ministry* (Downers Grove: Intervarsity Press, 1995), 52. See also Kadi Cole, *Developing Female Leaders: Navigate the Minefields and Release the Potential of Women in Your Church* (Nashville: Thomas Nelson, 2019), 52–53.

leadership. It also had a history of wars between the pastors and the congregation, the latest one resulting in the pastor leaving with half of the congregation in tow. History demonstrates the reason why the call for the role of senior pastor was given to me.

The shock of the assignment of a female senior pastor drew the attention of the provincial paper, *The Montreal Gazette*. After they reported on the story, God used the article as the tool to give the congregation positive notoriety, resulting in growth at Bible Way Church. Demonstrating a tough leadership stance, we made significant repairs to the building. The congregation grew exponentially, and the financial viability of the church returned. After two years, I decided to hand the leadership over to a young male pastor and responded to the burning call to become an evangelist who would go to the nations.

In 1998, God inspired me to begin an evangelistic ministry called Foundations Ministries. This ministry enabled me to travel for 20 years, ministering in over 29 countries. Foundations Ministries operated under a broad umbrella, which allowed me to work as an evangelist within my denomination but also with several other denominations worldwide. For about 12 weeks of each year I worked internationally as an evangelist, in the full sense of the definition. The rest of my time was spent within North America as a revivalist. Living the life of an evangelist was elating and fulfilling. Recognizing its fruitfulness still brings great joy to my heart.

DEAL WITH UNRESOLVED FEELINGS

Once when travelling in South Africa, I had the opportunity to get across the rough Atlantic waters outside of Cape Town over to the infamous Robben Island, known for its history of imprisoning mainly political dissidents, such as Nelson Mandela. Interestingly, today the prison tour is given by former political prisoners whose lives were ravaged on this same Robben Island during the reign of apartheid.

I joined a group of tourists for a prison tour. Our excellent guide, Jama, challenged our worldview as he took us through the prison. He was the most gracious, kind, gentle man you could ever meet. Jama was very soft-spoken, very respectful, and extremely diplomatic. His steps ahead of us caused us all to pause and simply observe him walking through the halls of the same prison where he was held captive for 21 years. His life lessons were riveted into our spirits, and you could hear a pin drop whenever he began to speak. During apartheid, Jama's perceived crime (and the reason he was sent to prison) was that he, as a young student in 1976, had organized his school's protest against the Bantu education law.

The tour was chilling! But a life-transforming moment of encouragement came after a tourist made an astonishingly foolish statement. She asked a very insensitive question regarding the extremely oppressive plight that Jama had just suffered for over 20 years of his life. The entire tour group became slightly annoyed; hence I tried to ease the tension by asking Jama this question: "What is it that bothers you the most now?" Jama's answer, spoken with comfort and confidence, was this: "With so much of my life taken away because of evil and hate, I have learnt to never let anything offend me that will take another moment from my life."

Jama's answer penetrated my heart! Since then, his words have reshaped my perspective when people either offend or hurt me because of my colour, culture, or femininity. Jama's well-spoken words beautifully illustrated this Scripture verse: "Make allowance for each other's faults, and forgive anyone who offends you. Remember, the Lord forgave you, so you must forgive others" (Col. 3:13 NLT).

BE UNHINDERED BY YOUR FEMININITY

While women leaders have faced great difficulty in preaching ministries in previous times, I remain thankful that much of what God has called me to accomplish has occurred in this age of modernity. During my tenure of ministry, a few men have occasionally made some negative comments to me; however, others have responded positively to the strength of my ministry. Many have taken note of the accomplishments rather than my femininity. On a humorous note, I must confess that the only time I saw my own limitations as a woman was during a baptismal service when I lacked the physical strength to pull up a sizable lady after lowering her into the baptismal tank. A humorous moment that ended well.

However, it has been alarming to recognize the number of people who still maintain jaded views of women in ministry. One example of this worldview occurred when I served as a camp speaker. Summer camp meetings are an exciting venue for both pastor and parishioners to find a time and place for spiritual refreshing. On multiple occasions, I was alarmed at the glaring difference in treatment between myself and my counterpart—a male speaker. On one occasion, I was given a cabin that had no drinking water placed in it, yet the leadership forgot to inform me that the running water in the cabin was not drinkable. Another time, for two days the camp administration forgot that they had not made any provision for me to have lunch (while no meal plan was available during the day in their cafeteria), and I had no provision of a car, as this luxury would not be repaid by the camp officials. However, when the male minister sharing the speaking schedule with me arrived, he was provided with a car for accessibility, a warning about the water issue, and an immediate offer to be taken out for lunch.

At yet another camp, from which I later shook the dust off my feet, again there was no provision of drinking water in the cabin or during the services, and this was during an intensely hot summer. However, the male speaker was doted over and introduced in the service with many accolades. My introduction to the congregation was given by the worship leader, who simply nodded to me, indicating that I should come and take the microphone now. Such glaring contrasts in treatment made me very aware that these incidents were simply from a disregard for the equality of women. The question now arises: "How did I deal with these situations mentioned here?" The answer is that I simply preached harder, loved on the people more, and demonstrated that I could not be brought to despair but instead would minister under God's anointing and send the people home charged in his presence. Remaining unhindered means taking the situation in stride and rising above it. So I worked harder!

BE UNRESTRICTED BY YOUR STATUS

One who is both single and a woman faces great opposition within the predominantly complementarianism mentality that exists in ministry. As a strong single woman who remained focused in her call, I recognized that I had seemingly intimidated many. Nevertheless, it was easy to take comfort from the Word of God. Throughout the Bible and in history, powerful women have always existed and have accomplished great works. The Bible lists women who are noted for travelling for God. Revival movements in past decades welcomed great women preachers, whether single or married. Only after institutionalization did the honour given such women change. As a result, neither the role of an evangelist nor the call to travel is new to single women.

It became extremely necessary for me, in my years as an evangelist, to coin many phrases to respond to folks who consistently joked at or queried me on my singleness. Statements such as these became my default response in varied situations:

- "I am still single because your prayers have not been strong enough to pray in my husband."
- "According to the faith of your prayers, that mighty man will become a reality."
- "I have not yet married or carried, so not ready to be buried—there's still time."
- "No one should be penalized for exercising wisdom when it was necessary."

With almost three decades of preaching ministry behind me, I have seen God confirm not only his call but also his commission upon my life in every conceivable capacity. Therefore, I resolve to continue to seek God's anointing upon my life by living for the demonstration of Christ's power being made manifest wherever he sends me. In this decade, his explicit call on my life is to contend for the baptism of the Holy Spirit in the midst of our churches. I must remind myself precisely why I do what I do: I am called of God; I have been set apart by God; and I have been given his Word to preach to the people of the world, reminding all that freedom comes through the Lord Jesus Christ.

FINAL WORDS

I have based my life's call and journey on these four fundamentals and have been unrelenting and uncompromising in fulfilling them:

- As an evangelist—to see more believers saved, healed, and delivered.
- As a revivalist—to see more believers renewed in their relationship with Christ.

- As a current lead pastor—to see more souls saved.
- As a called-out one—to be sensible about the times and remind people of Jesus' imminent return.

Our duty to God cannot be adjusted because of the treatment of humans. Persevering has not only made me stronger and bolder, but I believe it has also broken the barriers that our human systems establish to entrap those who do not fit what is considered "the norm," and it has created a greater system of acceptance of my gifts as a woman and an acknowledgement of what women can do in ministry. Being a part of the consistent catalyst for change has been a joy, not drudgery. My continuous goal is to ensure that no woman, young or old, will ever have to suffer what I have suffered, because after I have suffered through it, I intend to see it changed. That's the leadership I advocate!

In this overview of what I consider to be a very colourful and incredibly blessed life, the lessons learnt are simple but life-giving. By conducting some of these basic principles in your life, you will give yourself the licence to succeed, regardless of what life throws at you. So carefully understand the past, deliberately practice unwavering faith, graciously embrace the unchangeable examples, with determination be unbending in the call, patiently be understanding of process, be resolutely unashamed of your calling, and confidently be unaffected by others' misconceptions. Above all this, recognize God's plan over your life and just live it out by his Spirit's empowerment.

Serving in Song and Support

Ruth Ann Onley

I n a million years, I would never have dreamed of being called "Your Honour" or having a secret code name—"Songbird"—used by the Ontario Provincial Police, but I did! For seven amazing years I would be involved in a unique kind of "Kingdom work," one that involved a queen named Elizabeth and her royal kingdom. Who dreams up stuff like that? God does! My husband was appointed as the Queen's representative in Ontario and became the 28th lieutenant governor (LG) of Ontario on September 5, 2007. It was a vice-regal role, and I came with him!

We would travel to Beijing, London, Guadalajara, and Vancouver for the Paralympic Games, cheering on our blade runners and sledge hockey players. We would visit the sick and remember the dead. There would be saluting honour guards, community social events of celebration, and thousands of award ceremonies for Ontarians of all ages. We would dine with queens and princesses, emperors and ambassadors, presidents and prime ministers. It would be a storybook I had never opened before, wrapped in tight ribbons of protocol.

How does God put together a script like that? The answer is found in his Word: "Only I can tell you the future before it even happens. Everything I plan will come to pass, for I do whatever I wish" (Isa. 46:10 NLT).

If I could pick one song to sing about my life, it would be "Story of My Life":

> You are the story of my life
> I need You by my side both now and ever
> You are the lover of my soul
> No matter where I go, I know it's true
> The story of my life is You.[14]

"Story of My Life" reminds me that each of us has a story to tell. Our chapters will be different and may include some plot twists that we could never have imagined. But, as this song tells us, God is the author of our stories. I see God's penmanship across every page of my life as I reflect on all the chapters written so far.

FAMILY LEGACY

I was born in Simcoe, Ontario, and raised on a 78-acre apple farm, originally settled by my father's family from Scotland. My father was a Royal Canadian Air Force air-sea rescue pilot in World War II. After the war, he built our home on my grandfather's farmland and became a part-time fruit grower and the assistant general manager of the Norfolk Co-Op. Dad was a warm and loving man who gave me bear hugs and told me I was the apple of his eye. I adored him.

My mother was an accomplished concert pianist who stayed at home to raise my two older brothers and me while teaching piano and organ in our home. I was very close to Mom and enjoyed being her little helper by preparing meals, cleaning the house, and ironing my dad's shirts for work. After school and throughout the evenings, as students waited for their piano lessons in our living room, I learned to cook dinner all by myself, using Mom's little notes of instruction to set the table, peel the potatoes, and cook the meat.

---

14. Shannon Wexelberg, "Story of My Life," track 6 on *Story of My Life*, Doxology Records, 2002, compact disc.

I was blessed to grow up in a loving middle-class Christian home, knowing the security of parents who loved each other and their children. And I knew God loved me. Every week we attended First Baptist Church, where my father taught Sunday school and Mom was the supply organist and my Canadian Girls in Training leader. Life revolved around our church.

At the age of 11, I asked Jesus into my heart and was baptized. My young heart was tender to God's first whispers, perhaps from the awareness of missionary grandparents and my faithful parents. Or perhaps it had something to do with my inner nature, which my mother described as quiet and reserved, sensitive and serious.

My decision to follow Christ was further revealed in my grade 4 art class when we were asked to draw what we would like to be when we grew up. I drew a picture of a prim and proper young lady wearing a hat and carrying her purse in one hand and her Bible in the other. Underneath I printed, "I would like to be a missionary." I have since banished the missionary stereotypes I held as a child and have come to realize that if you are a follower of Christ, you are a missionary everywhere! No hat, purse, or sometimes even Bible required! All that is needed for God to accomplish his purposes is our heart and a willing mouth to testify in word and song. Psalm 139:13–14 tells us we are God-crafted: "For you created my inmost being; you knit me together in my mother's womb. I praise you because I am fearfully and wonderfully made; your works are wonderful, I know that full well."

I wasn't a perfect child. A particular instance of naughtiness has stuck in my memory throughout the years. One time, as a five-year-old kindergarten student, I gathered with my class in a semi-circle to sing "God Save the Queen," accompanied by our teacher, Miss Masson. (This was before "O Canada" became our official national anthem.) While Miss Masson was playing the piano, I decided to talk to Herbert, the boy standing beside me, instead of sing. Suddenly, the music stopped as Miss Masson rose from the piano bench. She strode over to her desk, pulled out a ruler, and marched straight back to me. Three good whacks on my hand later, I tearfully sang my way through the anthem.

Years later, I found myself standing beside Prince Charles in the lieutenant governor's office, heartily leading in the singing of "God Save the Queen," facing Her Majesty's official portrait. I did this for hundreds of official events, sometimes emotionally choking back tears as I thought about how our loving God could use a disobedient little girl, who had wanted to be a missionary, to sing his almighty name in the public forum.

WORDS OF AFFIRMATION

My mother was my music mentor and started teaching me piano from the time I was five years old. I admired her amazing ability and wanted to play the piano just like her. But as much as I wanted to excel at piano, my true passion was singing. Listening to my parents' record albums on the stereo, I would meticulously study every vocal nuance of the popular singers of the day.

Every Saturday night, my mom and dad and I gathered around the TV, watching *The Lawrence Welk Show*. Usually, I sat under the hair dryer because the next day was church and my hair had to be clean and curled. With my ears poking out from under the scratchy plastic bonnet, I didn't miss a note as I listened to the girls sing. I wanted to be a Welk girl so badly and to sing just like Norma Zimmer, who had a beautiful, sweet, bell-like voice.

However, I diligently practised and passed my Royal Conservatory piano exam pieces year after year until grade 10. One day, in the middle of practising some very difficult arpeggio scales, I slumped over the keys and cried out with sobbing wails, "I don't want to do this anymore. I hate playing piano!" I finally worked up the courage to tell Mom that I just didn't have the same love for the piano as she did and I did not want to continue. Mom then said something that would impact my life forever. She told me that I did not have natural musical skill with my fingers, but I did have it with my voice: a natural, God-given voice.

This was the moment when I knew in my heart that I wanted to sing for the rest of my life. With Mother's words inspiring my heart and fuelling my passion to sing, I began serious vocal training and never looked back. I began to sing at church, at weddings, in my high school choir, and in local musical theatre. I loved it all! God used a mother's wisdom and words of affirmation to set my feet on a new path, which would eventually glorify his name in song.

All throughout high school I had a vocal coach named Harry, who smoked like a chimney! I reeked of smoke after every lesson. (This was in the '60s when smoking was permitted everywhere, even during my singing lessons! To this day, I thank God for his protection from the second-hand smoke I endured during the many years of nightclub singing later in my career.)

Ironically, it was Harry who taught me an important breathing technique. Lying on my back on the floor with Webster's dictionaries piled high on my chest, I would inhale deeply from my diaphragm, watching the books rise and then fall as I exhaled. When my diaphragm reached its maximum height, I would hold my breath and count as long as I could. Most of the time the books came tumbling down, which would make me laugh. I hated doing these exercises, but they strengthened my diaphragm and prevented me from the dreaded habit of singing with my throat. Harry was not a religious man, but he would look me in the eye with tears in his own and say, "Ruth, you have 'it'—whatever 'it' is."

I loved Harry deeply, and I knew he believed in me. As great mentors and teachers do, Harry's words would inspire me to continue forward on a yet unknown musical path. I have always believed that "it" was God's special anointed gift of a singing voice, a talent to be used for his glory. For many years after Harry's lessons, I would sing secular music filled with emotion and passion. But after my secular singing career, when I decided to sing about God's transforming love through Jesus, my voice would become an instrument of praise to the Almighty God, and he would become my audience of one.

MY PARENTS' PLAN: A FOUR-YEAR UNIVERSITY DEGREE

After high school, having passed the dreaded grade 13 chemistry and physics prerequisites, I was accepted into the consecutive four-year home economics program at Guelph University. My parents thought home economics would be a great career choice since I loved sewing, something Mom had taught me to do. Also, my father had studied at Guelph in the Aggie (agricultural) program before the war.

Why didn't I choose to study music? I had never been interested in pursuing a classical music degree. But deep within, I was impatient to discover the world of professional singing. I just wanted to sing. One month before university began, I made a decision that would change my life course. I switched from home economics to a bachelor of arts in psychology and French. This program operated on the semester system, which meant I could take a term off at any time and continue the following term.

After two years of university studies, I was struggling, discouraged, and disconnected from campus life. I was not happy and not interested in continuing for a third year. That summer I sent out demo tapes to music agencies and received a call from Toronto to join a Canadian pop band that would tour the US. I was asked to be one of two female backup singers with four band musicians. Excited, I convinced my parents that I should try out this singing opportunity. After all, I could always return to the semester system at university and complete my degree. (But I never did!)

MY PLAN: A PROFESSIONAL SINGING CAREER

Touring in a singing group was new and exciting. I enjoyed learning new songs and simple dance routines. But after three years, the adventures of my non-stop travelling band life wore off, and for the next five years I settled in Toronto as a single, self-employed musician. My cousin and I shared an apartment, and my singing work consisted of performing at dinner clubs, stage shows, conventions, weddings, or on television—any opportunity that would pay the rent.

Laryngitis and second-hand smoke constantly wreaked havoc on my singing voice. The lifestyle of singing late hours and the darkness of the night-life work environment pulled my soul down into a place I didn't want it to be. All throughout my twenties, I chose to live life "My Way," just like the popular song I sang. I pushed God neatly to the sidelines and thought I would call on him whenever I chose. After all, I was from a good Christian home, baptized at the age of 11, and not living a riotous life or into the drug scene. I just didn't want to be perceived as religious in my singing career as I thought it might limit my future in the music business. I had lost my way. But God hadn't gone anywhere, and he was about to get my attention.

GOD'S PLAN TO CONQUER MY HEART

One night while I was rushing to get to work singing at an airport hotel, a young man knocked on our apartment door. He had a pleasant face, a lovely smile, and a cane in his hand. He politely asked for my cousin and told me they were work colleagues planning a promotion strategy for the release of his space novel, *Shuttle*. The young man's name was David Onley. Brushing him aside, I quickly dashed off to work.

David reappeared several weeks later and invited my cousin and me to go to his church. It was a large downtown church in Toronto, known to have many eligible bachelors in attendance. That caught my attention! After the service, David introduced us to a group of young people, and we all went out for lunch.

I continued going to church and then out to lunch. Two of the girls began telling me about their lives and poured out their faith stories. Judith was self-employed and ran her own beauty business. I could relate to her. Dianne had been involved in wrong relationships for many years. I could relate to her also. Both girls told me about Jesus coming into their hearts and changing everything in their lives. I knew about this Jesus they were talking about from my Christian upbringing. But I didn't know Jesus the way they did. I wanted what they both had with him: a living relationship and one that would transform my life. But was I willing to surrender control of my life to Christ?

The next Sunday after church, we went to Dianne's apartment, and over apricot tea Dianne asked me if I would like to invite Christ into my life and allow him take over the controls of my life. Tears flooded from my eyes as I asked God to forgive my stubborn heart and take over the controls. For so many years I had sung the popular hit song "My Way." Now I wanted God to lead my life his way. Years later, it was no coincidence that my first Christian CD would be entitled *The Way*. In John 14:6, Jesus said, "I am the way, the truth and the life: no man cometh unto the Father, but by me" (KJV).

After accepting Christ, I felt a peace unlike anything I had experienced. Jesus was living inside me, never to leave me or forsake me. My life changed forever, and I hungered to know him more. After my decision to follow Christ, I made another choice: to stop seeing the man I had been dating. The Holy Spirit was at work.

Over the next few months, I began to see David at casual events with our church friends and over dinner. I considered him my "spiritual mentor friend" and not really my date. It was also during this time period that I turned to country music, hired a new manager, and recorded my first two singles, which did well on the music charts. So much was happening at once, and I thought God was finally unfolding his will for me: a career in country music.

LISTENING TO GOD'S VOICE

I thought David was handsome and unlike anyone I had ever met. He was smart, articulate, and creative and knew something about almost any subject. I was drawn, above all, to his deep Christian faith, something I had not found in anyone I had dated. But there was one thing about David I wasn't sure I wanted to face: he had polio. Since the age of three David had battled with this disease. He wore full leg braces, carried a cane, and walked with an unusual gait. I never thought my Prince Charming would be disabled.

Then God gave me a wake-up call. One night, I bolted straight up in my bed. I was jolted awake by the sound of my own voice yelling, "No! No! No!" Three times I heard a voice saying, "Ruth, you're going to marry him!" and three times I yelled back, "No!" I knew I was responding to God's voice telling me that I would marry David. But my plan was always to marry another musician, to be a team, and to ride off into the sunset like Roy Rogers and Dale Evans! I had grown up with a cousin who had been born with cerebral palsy, and I knew the difficulties faced by his family, so I had never envisioned myself marrying someone with a physical disability. But sometimes God has to get our attention in dramatic ways to show us his plans, even marriage plans!

God was in control of my life, and I decided I would trust him. Seven months after surrendering my life to Christ with an unquenchable thirst to know him better, I surrendered my heart to David with an overflowing love beyond understanding. I was drawn to this man, David, unlike anyone I had ever met, and I knew I was in love with him. He asked me to marry him, and I replied, "Yes!" I took a huge leap of faith into marriage and the world of disability. I would trust God's plan.

TRUSTING GOD'S PLAN

Our marriage started off in a most untraditional way: living on a small advancement for David's book, which had just launched. We didn't have enough money to keep an apartment, so we lived with David's parents. I continued my singing career, and David joined me on the road in his 1974 Buick, following behind my band truck, which was loaded with sound equipment. The country music clubs that we toured ranged from fine hotels to beer-stained dives (in the music business, it's called "paying your dues"). From coast to coast, we got to know Canadians from every walk of life who loved their country and their country music. But beyond the music and laughter, I also saw the dark side of alcohol. And it was sobering, indeed.

Having a political science degree but being unsuccessful in obtaining a full-time job, David honed his skills as a writer, submitting newspaper articles and recording weekly radio reports for CFRB back in Toronto, while I sang, using my paycheques to pay off equipment and truck loans. David's love and support encouraged me to follow my dreams. In 1982 I won "Newcomer of the Year Award" in Canadian country music and recorded an album with MCA in Nashville and Los Angeles. We were certain that God was unfolding his music plan, and it seemed so promising!

One year into our travelling marriage, God surprised us with his new family plan. I was pregnant. I had always wanted to have a family eventually, but not now! This announcement was "bad news and bad timing," for the record company then immediately dropped my contract. I was conflicted, musically devastated and baby-elated at the same time. What was God doing? I struggled with Jeremiah 29:11: "'For I know the plans I have for you,' declares the LORD, 'plans to prosper you and not to harm you, plans to give you hope and a future.'" I loved singing and I loved my baby. I wanted both, or so I thought.

Three months after our son Jonathan was born, I returned to singing with my band. Both of my dear parents joined me on the road and took turns babysitting as I sang late into the night. I later hired a young nanny to travel with me, but that soon made me feel uncomfortable. David frequently stayed back in Toronto doing radio work. Juggling our careers and family life became a complicated logistical nightmare, and I was totally exhausted. I finally waved the white flag and surrendered. My season for singing had come to an end, and I entered into a fallow season. God was preparing a new work ahead, and I would learn to rest in his plan.

Over the next few years, my late-night singing in country music clubs was replaced by late-night feedings and whispered lullabies as our family expanded to include three healthy rambunctious little boys sharing one bedroom in our downtown apartment. David was now fully employed as a broadcaster at Citytv, becoming the first Canadian broadcaster with a physical disability on television. When he wasn't doing the news, David spent hours on the phone answering calls and trying to help solve the unbelievable problems encountered by people with disabilities in the community. We thanked God for this job. David would later make good his heart-held vow to help improve the lives of people living with disability, and God would provide the way in the form of a new job.

MINISTRY AT HOME

I loved my boys, and I loved motherhood: a daily off-stage performance of laundry and diapers, accompanied by the never-ending commotion from my trio of testosterone-laden boys. The sound of music, however, was being slowly stifled deep within my soul. Busy at home as I was, I missed singing.

One day someone from our church gave me a cassette of a Christian singer named Sandy Patti. Coming from a Convention Baptist church background, I had never even heard this kind of Christian music. Sandy Patti was part of the explosion of American gospel music in the 1980s, which also included big-name singers like Larnelle Harris and Steve Green. David and I decided to see Sandy Patti in concert at Maple Leaf Gardens. As I listened to her powerfully anointed voice, God spoke to me, and I made another decision that would turn the course of my life: I would sing for God's glory, and it would be Christ's music, not country music!

I recorded a demo tape of my singing and sent it to the music directors of Peoples Church in Toronto and *100 Huntley Street*, Canada's daily Christian television show. Both invited me to sing on their programs, and with the outreach of their television broadcasts, a new music ministry began as bookings soon came in from churches, women's ministries, and conference centres all across Canada.

The kitchen became my singing studio and the stage where I rehearsed songs, playing accompaniment tracks on my counter stereo. With constant interruptions by our busy boys, I pressed on practising.

David has always reminded me that throughout the years, my singing and rehearsing has brought encouragement to his heart in moments he needed it most. Sometimes there were tears in his eyes.

When our first son, Jonathan, was very young, he would often send me off on my singing engagements with his cheerful words "Mommy, are you going to sing to the Lord?" ("Sing to the Lord" was the first song I recorded on my demo tape, and he had heard it endlessly.) God taught me early on that our greatest ministry first starts at home where little eyes and ears are watching and listening. Charles H. Spurgeon says it best: "You are as much serving God in looking after your own children, and training them up in God's fear, and minding the house, and making your household a church for God as you would be if you had been called to lead an army to battle for the Lord of Hosts."[15]

The sound of music was back in my soul, and I loved to proclaim God's truth in song. I tried to make sure each song contained lyrics that were scripturally based with the clear gospel of Jesus Christ. With the family's love and support, I continued singing and also became involved in the leadership of Christian Women's Club and Community Bible Study. We thanked God for his provision and blessings. Life was absolutely at full throttle with our three healthy, active, growing boys. I continued to pray, "Lord, please let my life be lived, if not for income, then for outcome."

LEADERS NEED SPIRITUAL MENTORS

I thank God for the older women who mentored me while I raised my children and who continue to inspire me today. I call them my spiritual mothers.

Ethel, one of the founders of Christian Women's Club, encouraged me to serve in several leadership roles with her ministry. For many years, I travelled in Canada and the US, giving my testimony and singing for these wonderful Christian outreach meetings. Ethel has also led countless mission trips around the world, and I joined her recently to go to Italy to teach singing in a Nigerian refugee children's ministry. Now a dynamic 92-year-old, Ethel is still leading mission teams, and I am excited to again this summer be a part of her mission team to Peru.

---

15. Charles H. Spurgeon, "Strengthening Medicine for God's Servants," *The Metropolitan Tabernacle Pulpit* 21, no. 1214 (London: Passmore & Alabaster, 1875), 52–53.

I am still in touch with Wilma, my grade 3 Bible teacher, who drilled her students in Scripture memorization and today, at 94, still encourages me to teach my grandchildren Scriptures. I know today that the Scriptures imbedded in my memory all these years later are there because of Wilma's faithful teaching of Scripture memorization. My 55-year-old neon-orange ruler with the books of the Bible written on it still reminds me of the incentive I had to memorize Scripture in Wilma's class!

Dorothy, now 88 years young, was teaching director and one of the founders of Community Bible Study, Scarborough. She encouraged me to become a core leader and taught me that prayer is the key foundation of all we plan or do. I will never forget Tuesday mornings as our leadership team sat in a small, tight circle, almost knee-to-knee, praying together for the Bible study meeting on Wednesday. Dorothy was a prayer warrior who opened her heart to God. Her authenticity and vulnerability impacted my own prayer life. Like me, Dorothy also raised three sons, and I loved hearing her personal stories as our teaching director about her children as she explained our Bible study lessons each week using her own family stories—the good and the bad. I could relate so well!

There are so many older women in my path today whose godly wisdom and experience I value greatly. All of them are now well into their senior years, but God has taught me that age does not define our ability to minister the gospel effectively; nor does it diminish all he has called (and equipped) us to be. Our age does not define who we are.

Many years ago, as a young person, I heard a voice deep within my soul saying to me, "When you're older, Ruth, when you're older!" I could never really understand what was going to happen when this "older" me occurred. Today, I believe it was God's voice reassuring my then youthful soul that he was with me and that he would be with me in my older years as my life experiences became bigger, fuller, and maybe even a little harder to imagine!

GOD'S SURPRISING CALL TO SERVICE

It was Victoria Day 2006. The boys, now grown and home from university for the holiday weekend, had just left the table, and with the dinner dishes cleared, I sat down to catch up with David's day in the newsroom. By the look on his face, I knew something was up. Nervously clearing his throat,

David looked at me and said that he had been asked to consider putting his name forward to become the next lieutenant governor of Ontario. He said it would be a federal appointment and decided by the prime minister.

David asked me what I thought. My eyes popped with surprise, and my first thought was "What exactly does a lieutenant governor do?" But in reality, because of David's job as a reporter for Citytv, we had gone to many social events where the LG was in attendance. I knew that this person represented the Queen in each province, but that was all.

My immediate response to David's question was "Yes, absolutely! I think you should go for it!" (Later David told me he was quite surprised at my enthusiastic response.) We both felt that David's background in political science and politics as well as his television experience technically qualified him for the position. But was our prime minister ready and willing to put someone with a physical disability into this position?

LEADERS WAIT IN THE PRAYER ROOM

We were told that speaking publicly about David's decision to put his name forward would end any chance for him to become the next LG of Ontario. We told no one, not even our three sons. Our code word about any developing details became "the project." We prayed endlessly all summer for God to reveal his will for David's life, and on a Sunday in September God answered. While sitting in church, David felt a chill running up his spine. He heard God's voice saying to him, "You will be lieutenant governor, and you shall be my servant." The next day, David agreed to let his name stand. "The project" remained secret from our family and friends for an entire year as key people submitted confidential letters of endorsement for David.

In November 2006, I received a call to sing "O Canada" at the LG's suite. I could hardly contain myself as I sang and smiled broadly at the current LG. At the reception following the event, I mingled amongst the guests but kept striking up conversations with the aides-de-camp, attendants to the LG. I pressed them discreetly with questions about the duties of the LG and his wife. My head was spinning with every detail and overwhelmed with the amazing words and information I was told. I remembered what David had told me with his delightful humour just before I had headed out the door to sing that day: "Have a great time,

Ruth; just don't get caught measuring the curtains!" (Ironically, on day two after David's installation as LG, I was approached with fabric samples to pick out new chair coverings!)

For a total of 14 months, David and I sat on our secret, praying and trusting God for his purpose to unfold. Either way, we knew God was in charge of our future plans, and we would put our trust and faith in the fact that our sovereign God knows what his best is for us. We had heard that David was one of two candidates for the final pick and were at peace either way.

In July 2007, David finally received the phone call he had been praying about. While he was driving up the Don Valley Parkway, with a warm summer rain lightly falling on the windshield, his car phone rang. It was Prime Minister Stephen Harper. The two talked for 20 minutes, and David got the job! We were told our lives would change forever.

The entire summer was spent poring over six huge black binders and being oriented to David's work. It became known as LG summer school! Each day our garage door would open as a shiny black Honda Odyssey driven by two OPP officers pulled in to pick us up. It was now a new reality for the incumbent LG to be protected by a security team that would stay with him for his entire term. David was forbidden to drive, even for personal use. No matter where he went in public, from shopping malls to our home church, David had two OPP officers with him. It was different for the spouse. I could drive to wherever I needed. Only when I was with David did security apply to me as well.

"FOR SUCH A TIME AS THIS"

On September 5, 2007, David was installed as the 28th lieutenant governor of Ontario. It was a grand public occasion with the governor general's horse guards, pipers, gun salutes, and prayer by our pastor in the legislature. A wonderful reception was held afterward for family and friends.

When the last guest departed, I walked to the main door and gazed, exhausted, outside its window. What a surreal day! Suddenly, within our room, I repeatedly heard, "Your Honour, Your Honour." It kept going. I was thinking, "David, for Pete's sake, answer this poor man!" Exasperated, I spun around to search for David but instead found the chief steward looking at me, not David! "Your Honour" became my official title for the next seven years. Early on, I asked David's chief of staff if I could just be referred to as Ruth Ann. She simply replied, "No, Your Honour!" I was to learn that officially I had no constitutional authority, but historically the honorific title was also given to the spouse of the LG. It made me feel very uncomfortable, and it took some time for me to truly feel at ease being addressed this way.

As the constitutional head of the provincial government, David's role was to sign thousands of official documents before they became law. In addition to the official and social functions representing the Queen in the province, each LG has a personal mandate that focuses attention on a specific public concern in Ontario. David's mandate was to promote accessibility for the disabled and Aboriginal literacy in the Far North (carried forward from his predecessor). He defined accessibility as "that which enables people to achieve their full potential." David's unwavering passion to change attitudes and erase stigma attached to the disabled weighed heavily on his shoulders throughout his term and continues today.

LEADERS MUST STEP OUTSIDE THEIR COMFORT ZONES

Because there is no official role or staff for the spouse of the LG, I was told I could decide how much I wanted to be involved in David's work. I chose to simply support David in whatever way I could. Little did I know how much work was ahead of me and how far I would be pushed outside of my comfort zone!

My first challenge was to help David to reach the communities in the Far North. Because David was unable to get into the small twin-engine government plane used by the LG and the premier, and because the northern terrain was too rough to navigate by scooter, I was asked to visit the northern communities on David's behalf. I knew that if I didn't go, the Aboriginal literacy program might not continue. So I went.

Over the next seven years, I flew into 23 communities, visiting schools and talking to the band chiefs about children's literacy and community needs. Sometimes I visited isolated communities devastated by teen suicides; other times I visited the children's summer literacy camps run by David's office. Every trip was emotionally wrenching and physically exhausting, as we covered several communities per trip, landing on gravel runways and pressed by tight schedules. In all of these unknown and sometimes very difficult situations, I discovered that I needed to trust God to give me the right words to speak and the wisdom to be silent. I learned to depend on God for his protection and safety as we flew over remote forests and lakes in weather conditions that changed by the minute. As I prayed for discernment for our two pilots, God's peace flooded my soul, and I knew my Great Pilot was in control and all would be well.

Grand Chief Stan Beardy was a fervent Christian and would often join me on these trips. He taught me to sing "Amazing Grace" and "How Great Thou Art" in Oji Cree and would always insist that I sing them wherever we landed. On one of those occasions, a row of elder women sat weeping as I sang. Surely the presence of the Lord was in that place. Surrounded by so many symbols of Aboriginal culture, I was moved by the love of Jesus in the hearts of those women.

On my final trip north in September 2014, I was joined by Sophie, the Countess of Wessex (married to the Queen's youngest son, Edward), Premier Kathleen Wynne, and Elizabeth Dowdeswell, the LG designate. I will never forget the countess's speech as she talked about the Great White Mother who cared about the people of the Far North. Aboriginal people know the historic connection between their treaties and the Queen. Tears of affection flowed from the crowd as the countess spoke to their hearts. I felt honoured to have been given the opportunity to serve the northern communities for seven years.

With my limited knowledge of Aboriginal culture and politics, I am grateful to God for pushing me out of my comfort zone and into the unknown. Isaiah 40:31 best expresses my heart: "But they that wait upon the Lord shall renew their strength; they shall mount up with wings as eagles; they shall run, and not be weary; and they shall walk, and not faint" (KJV). These trips had significant and symbolic meaning to the Aboriginal ties to the Crown. My leadership in this role was not about exerting political power. Rather, by his strength, God enabled me to listen, support, and care for these people who had so little yet so generously gave of their kindness and hospitality. My presence there, in representing David and the province, reassured the people of the North that they, and especially their children, were not forgotten.

GRACE IN SERVING

One of the highlights of David's seven-year term was our opportunity to meet the Queen. On October 15, 2008, at noon, we were escorted into Buckingham Palace and seated in the grand red carpeted hallway. The Queen's lady-in-waiting sat with us, assuring us that the Queen would make us feel very comfortable. She warned us of only one thing—to let the Queen take the lead in all our conversations. As I listened, I was mesmerized by the huge oil paintings lining the long hallway—all splendid portraits of the royal family throughout the centuries. In a brain giggle, I thought about our sons' Sears portraits hanging in the hallway back home. Then, at the sound of a buzzer, we saw the huge double doors open, and there she stood, our gracious Queen, wearing a stunning silk emerald-green dress and a radiant smile.

My heart jumped as I shook the Queen's hand and did a wobbly curtsy, erasing weeks of curtsy protocol practice. Seated on his polished scooter, David did his neck bow flawlessly! Standing unobtrusively nearby, a young man in an air force uniform quickly snapped one candid official picture and then left. We were totally alone with the Queen.

Elizabeth II was exactly the woman we see in all the photos: very petite with a brilliant smile and perfectly coiffed white hair. She gestured toward three chairs arranged for conversation. David rolled his scooter into the empty fourth space. The Queen took my chair and slightly repositioned it for me, plumping the seat cushion with her hand. I could not believe my eyes and can only hope my mouth was not hanging open! On one of the chairs was an exquisite oil painting of two polar bears, painted by a Canadian disabled "mouth artist." It was the gift we had given Her Majesty on behalf of the people of Ontario.

The Queen began the conversation by asking David about our federal election, which had been held the day before, because she had not yet heard the results. David, having been briefed that morning from Canada, eagerly gave her a synopsis. The two continued talking with ease as the Queen asked about David's work with the disabled in Ontario. I had been listening intensely to their conversation, adding a few polite nods of affirmation from time to time. Then there was that moment when no one said a word. Looking straight into the Queen's eyes with a sudden, nervous arching of my back, I blurted out, "Your Majesty, your maple leaf brooch is very beautiful!" The Queen beamed and said, "Thank you very much. It was one of my mother's favourites." (We were later informed that the brooch had been given to the Queen Mother by Canada during the 1939 royal visit. Later that night in our hotel room, while watching the British news coverage, we noted that the Queen continued to wear the brooch at all her events that day.)

Although I had broken protocol by initiating conversation (reminiscent of the disobedient little kindergarten student who did not sing "God Save The Queen"), there was no royal whack on the knuckles given at the palace that day. We left convinced that the Queen had honoured our visit, and Canada, by wearing her maple leaf brooch, yet again showing her true bond of affection for our country. "God Save Our Gracious Queen" took on its truest meaning that day as I met a world leader who personified the word "grace."

The next time we met the Queen was in June 2010 when she visited Toronto and made her first-ever official visit to the LG suite. Keeping with tight, meticulously scripted protocol, David started to escort the Queen and introduce her in the manner she preferred to guests clustered in various groups and organizations. But Prince Philip stood still and did not go with her according to script. Turning to me and gesturing with an abrupt sweep of his hand toward a group of guests, Prince Philip exclaimed, "Well?" I quickly stepped up beside him, my heart pounding with embarrassment, and started introducing people to the duke. I fumbled at first but soon picked someone from each group to introduce the rest.

I learned a valuable lesson that day in public service: be prepared, do your homework, and watch out for curveballs. They will come! From then on, I always made sure I studied every detail of the itinerary schedule, knowing as much about the people and organizations as I could. It was challenging, but over time I became much more comfortable.

Something very meaningful occurred during our first visit with Prince Edward. David showed him an old black-and-white photo taken in 1959 of the Queen reviewing a group of children eagerly assembled together with a large banner overhead that read, "The crippled children of Toronto welcome ... our Queen." The children were all seated in wheelchairs, and in the very centre front row sat a nine-year-old boy named David Onley. It was a blistering hot day, but David was dressed in a wool suit and tie—a direct order from his British grandfather, who insisted upon his "proper attire"! Who could have imagined that 48 years later that same little boy in the photo would represent the Queen by becoming one of her lieutenant governors? God could!

After seeing the photo, Edward said, "As a little boy, I asked my mother, 'Mommy, why do we have children in wheelchairs in the front row?' She replied, 'So that everyone can see that they are people too.'" The Queen was making a public statement that everyone should have equal access to opportunity. These children in wheelchairs were brought outdoors to participate in a very special day like everyone else, and the Queen made sure of that.

Whenever I see the photo of the children in the wheelchairs, I am reminded of a song I sang in Sunday school called "When Mothers of Salem," based on the words of Matthew 19:14:

When mothers of Salem their children brought to Jesus,
The stern disciples drove them back and bade them to depart:
But Jesus saw them ere they fled and sweetly smiled and kindly said, "Suffer little children to come unto Me."
"For I will receive them and fold them to My bosom:
I'll be a shepherd to these lambs, O drive them not away;
For if their hearts to Me they give, they shall with Me in glory live:
Suffer little children to come unto Me."
How kind was our Saviour, to bid these children welcome!
But there are many thousands who have never learned His Name;
The Bible they have never read; They know not that the Saviour said, "Suffer little children to come unto Me."
O soon may the heathen of every tribe and nation
Fulfill Thy blessed word and cast their idols all away;
O shine upon them from above and show Thyself a God of love;
Teach the little children to come unto Thee.
(William Medlen Hutchings, 1850)

The Queen's gracious acceptance of people from every walk of life, whether rich, poor, young, old, or disabled, has been her living testimony throughout her entire life. Her leadership in her actions on the world stage has always spoken louder than her words.

LEADERS SERVE OTHERS WITH LOVE

One of my favourite books about the Queen was written as a tribute for Her Majesty's 90th birthday. It's called *The Servant Queen and the King She Serves*. One quote by royal biographer William Shawcross reflects my personal thoughts about the Queen best: "Two things stand out—the Queen's constant sense of duty and her devotion to God. Of this she speaks humbly but openly, especially in her Christmas broadcasts."[16] Not only was our royal Queen born as the daughter of King George VI; she is the royal daughter of the King of kings, adopted into his family by her professed faith in Christ. We are all daughters of the King when we confess Jesus as Lord and Saviour. We are then automatically adopted into his family for eternity. John 1:12 says, "But as many as received Him, to them He gave the right to become children of God, to those who believe in His name" (NKJV).

As followers of Christ, like the Queen, we become God's reflection to the world as we live out his words in John 15:12: "This is My commandment, that you love one another as I have loved you" (NKJV). But what does it mean to love one another? As Christian leaders, how do we practice loving others?

During David's term, I would often express to my husband how overwhelmed I felt by the "royal treatment," the "niceness beyond measure." All people should be treated as royally as we were, with kindness and dignity. I think the Queen feels the same way. She has shown love, compassion, and dignity to all people around the world, giving each one she meets the "royal treatment." Like the Queen, we can lead by example as we serve others with love.

BEING THE HANDS AND FEET OF JESUS

Throughout our marriage, I have tried to use my hands and feet in situations that were impossible for David. It was no different during his years as LG when I stepped in to fly north or to place medals around the necks of Paralympic athletes because he could not. David's needs are very specific and highly orchestrated. I have learned, through living with someone with a disability, that people with disabilities are huge problem solvers. Every single day they carve out a way to overcome one obstacle

---

16. Mark Greene and Catherine Butcher, *The Servant Queen and the King She Serves* (London: Bible Society, HOPE, London Institute for Contemporary Christianity, 2016), 2.

after another. David has been my greatest mentor, teaching me so much about persistence and resolve. He has often said that one of my pet sayings has been "It is what it is." And the truth about polio is—there is nothing we can do but live with it ... and pray!

One of the duties of the LG is to attend funerals of fallen police officers, military officers, firefighters, and government leaders. Accompanying David on each of these sad occasions, I would hug the grieving family members, whispering into their ears that we would be praying for them in the difficult days ahead. And we did. Seated on his scooter, David had limited arm strength and movement due to polio, and I knew he would have hugged if he could have.

While attending the funeral of former LG Lincoln Alexander, David spoke to the then governor general Michaëlle Jean and expressed how inadequate he felt on such occasions when trying to offer words of comfort. She replied, "They may not remember your words, but they will remember that you attended."

LEADING ON OUR KNEES

Polio has truly kept David and me on our knees, relying not on ourselves but on God's merciful hand of love to help us through very difficult times. Some days are plagued by post-polio fatigue, a sudden onset of extreme and debilitating fatigue. During David's LG years, there were many days when he had to push on through to complete his schedule, as "duty called." All David can do is stop, rest, and recharge, just like his mobile scooter, which requires daily battery charging. Each day, God is our source of strength. Jesus said, "My grace is sufficient for you, for My strength is made perfect in weakness" (2 Cor. 12:9 NKJV).

Prayer became the battery charger of David's years as LG of Ontario. Early every morning, we would have coffee together in our living room, calling it our personal "board meeting with God." We prayed over our children and family, our staff, our packed schedule, and for all the people we would meet that day. Deuteronomy 31:8 says, "The LORD himself goes before you and will be with you; he will never leave you nor forsake you. Do not be afraid; do not be discouraged."

During the years of David's term, many Christian believers would often tell us that they were praying for us. We received many notes of prayer encouragement. The Bible commands us to pray for those in authority in our country: "Pray ... for kings and all who are in authority so that we can live peaceful and quiet lives marked by godliness and dignity" (1 Tim. 2:2 NLT). We both appreciated and felt those prayers.

A song I often sing, "May I Be His Love for You" by Kathy Troccoli, expresses beautifully that truly we may be the only Jesus a person sees, as we reflect his love to them in our actions:

> May I be His love for you,
> May I lift your eyes towards heaven,
> May I call to you and lead you to His heart,
> May I cry His tears for you,
> May I be the place that you can run to
> Where you'll hear His voice
> And see Him with your eyes, all your life
> May I be His love.[17]

HE HOLDS MY HAND

On September 6, 2017, a "new little friend" came into my life—or rather literally into my heart—and I felt "born again" as a fresh wave of energy poured new life and vitality into me.

All summer I had been struggling with deep fatigue and found it difficult to keep up with normal living. I could barely lift the grocery bags without stopping to catch my breath, and I knew something was not right. Life felt stressed and strained, and I was out of breath, especially for singing, which became a chore. I wrestled inside to find the joy.

Several tests later and with a heartbeat well below normal, I had to trust God's medical experts. I needed a pacemaker immediately! Although my specialist reassured me that this was a very common procedure, I held a deep fear inside, knowing my parents' histories. My father had died hours after a heart attack and an emergency pacemaker surgery, and my mother's heart had stopped during a routine ultrasound. Both were my age when they died.

---

17. Kathy Troccoli, "May I Be His Love for You," track 9 on *Sounds of Heaven*, Reunion Records, 1995, compact disc. Quoted with permission.

Lying alone on a gurney, prepped for surgery and having had no food or water for 24 hours, I felt very weak and was getting weaker by the moment. I thought to myself, "So this is what dying feels like." I prayed continuously, trusting God to hold me in his love and to hold steady the hand of the young surgeon. God's absolute peace came over me like a heavy blanket. Fully awake during the one-hour procedure, I knew without a shadow of a doubt that the presence of the Great Healer was there.

As the surgery began, overhead music filled the room with the unmistakable rhythm and lyrics of a certain Bee Gees' song: "Aa, ha, ha, ha, stayin' alive, stayin' alive!" I couldn't believe my ears! At that moment I discovered that my God has a sense of humour. All would be well!

My sweet four-year-old granddaughter, Isabelle, always wants to see the scar from my surgery, which she calls "Nana's owie." The doctor has told me that my "owie" (my pacemaker) beats 100 percent of the time, not just when needed like some do. What a reminder that God's love is ever-present with us, 100 percent of the time. Psalm 27:14 says, "Wait for the LORD; be strong and take heart and wait for the LORD."

Christian leaders are not just those called to the pulpit or to high-profile public positions. God calls us all to lead wherever we are, to "bloom where we are planted." It only takes the light of one candle in one corner to light up an entire room. So trust God in your small corner, and go light your world!

I thank God for my faithful grade 2 Sunday school teacher. She was an old, short, grey-haired spinster by the name of Olive Green (yes, Olive Green!). She taught me the Lord's Prayer and this old children's hymn:

Jesus bids us shine
With a pure, clear light
Like a little candle
Burning in the night ...
He looks down from heaven
To see us shine
You in your small corner
And I in mine.
(Susan Warner [1819–1885])

Living the Unimaginable

Susan Finlay

"For we are God's handiwork, created in Christ Jesus to do good works, which God prepared in advance for us to do." (Eph. 2:10)

I t was doubtful that I would ever be born—at least in the minds of the medical community. After two miscarriages in two years, my mother was informed by medical specialists that in all probability she would be unable to ever carry a child to full term. For my parents, Leonard and Madeline Hultgren, determination fuelled by faith always overcame disappointments, of which they had their fair share. They modelled and instilled in me the belief that God is always greater than any circumstance, always wiser than the wisest of earthly wisdom.

MY HERITAGE: "EVEN IF" PEOPLE IN A "WHAT IF" WORLD

Eighteen months after the disappointing prognosis, I was born at Holy Cross Hospital in Calgary. Six and seven years later my two brothers, Peter and Rob, were born. We were now a family of five, living proof that we can never assume the limits of God's power or purposes.

When I was 10 months old, my parents faced another challenge: my father had accepted the call to pastor a church in Lethbridge, Alberta. The week we were to move from Calgary, Dad was diagnosed with tuberculosis. The customary treatment protocol of the time required many months in a sanatorium. So, instead of driving to Lethbridge, we flew to Hamilton, where we could live with my grandparents while Mom resumed her profession as a public health nurse and Dad spent the next 14 months in the Hamilton sanatorium. This life detour was pivotal for each of us.

Adaptability, humour, character development, pulling together, and rising above any experience were values that permeated our home. Dad used his time in the sanatorium to pursue doctoral courses through his alma mater, McMaster Divinity College. Mom was a model of a devoted wife and mother with a dedication to her vocation, instilling in me the importance of postsecondary education and pursuing a profession. She was a woman ahead of her time in many respects, which often proved challenging for her as a pastor's wife.

My mother certainly did not fit the stereotypical mould of the time; however, she was focused more on fulfilling the Lord's call and using the talents he had given her than on establishing a particular identity. A vibrant presence, Mom called life as it was, met life where it was, and had little tolerance for duplicity, contrivance, or affectation. At the same time, no one was more understanding, hospitable, or helpful to those in need, either physically or emotionally. As a public health nurse, Mom would go into some of the most challenging situations of neglect or abuse and was frequently called as a witness in court.

As a woman of quick mind and humour, Mom was characterized by determination; patience, less so. I still smile when I recall Mom telling me there was no such word as "can't." Puzzled by this, I asked my grade 1 teacher about it. On returning home, full of self-righteousness, I advised Mom that she was wrong; "can't" really was a word. Although I don't recall her specific reply, I recall with a smile her exasperated expression.

Psychologists tell us that "internal dialogue" has a profound impact for our good or to our detriment. A wise friend talks about the importance of changing the tape ("download") in our minds to reinforce the promises of God rather than reinforcing our worries, sense of inadequacy, and imaginings of prospective worst consequences. For me, one of the go-to tapes is "I can do all things through Christ who strengthens me" (Phil. 4:13 NKJV). There really is no such word as "can't" after all!

My paternal grandparents (Peter and Kristina Hultgren) and great-grandparents (Andrew and Lisa Hultgren) emigrated from Sweden to ultimately homestead in Midale, Saskatchewan, where Dad was born. He would say that his early years were filled with great loss, yet even greater love. When Dad was two years old, his mother and eight-year-old sister, Myrtle, died one day apart in the 1918 Spanish flu epidemic. Grandpa was now the single parent of six-year-old Ellen (a special needs child), five-year-old Arthur, two-year-old Leonard, and infant Gladys (who died three years later in 1921). Not until 1937 was Grandpa blessed to marry Florence and adopt her daughter, Ferne. Together they would know the joy of a baby daughter, Marilyn.

Such difficult situations often capsize people. I know second-hand how heartbreaking it was for Grandpa to lose his beloved wife and two young daughters. What I know first-hand is the character, faith, and transformative spirit that led him to become a respected community leader, serving as reeve/councillor for 27 years, founding chair of the hospital board, member of the regional health board and the credit union board, lay preacher, Bible teacher, and church trustee—all, of course, while farming.

Known as "Midale's dean in civic government," at 80 years of age Grandpa declined nomination for the civic election, believing the time had come to step aside for a younger person.[18] However, it was around this time that he personally built their final house in town. For Grandpa, also, there was no such word as "can't"!

One time, a couple of students passed Grandpa, saying, "Hello, old man." Rather than respond with a warranted reprimand, Grandpa walked into the school to suggest to the principal that an annual citizenship award be established. A great example of transformational leadership!

Although I never knew them, my paternal great-grandparents, Andrew and Lisa, had a profound impact on my life. In contributing to the book *Plowshares to Pumpjacks*, Dad wrote, "Andrew and Lisa contributed a rich legacy of qualities which have left their indelible imprint on their children and grandchildren ... Grandpa Andrew was a man of strong faith, hard work and vital prayer. When we came home late at night, we could pause outside his house and hear him praying for us."[19]

The power of a praying great-grandfather! It was said of Great-Grandfather Andrew that when he prayed, you believed that Jesus was sitting right across the table. Many have shared how he would "pray

18. *The Weyburn Review*, December 10, 1964, 8.
19. *Plowshares to Pumpjacks: R. M. of Cymri: Macoun, Midale, Halbrite* (Midale: R. M. of Cymri History Book Society, 1984), 323–324.

forward"—not only for the children and grandchildren he could see but also for generations not yet born. In a fast-food society of instant gratification, praying generations forward for those we do not know or see is a rare thing. The powerful impact of this was reinforced at a recent Hultgren family reunion as we celebrated with the many believers who also were current or former ministry leaders. How grateful I am for the prayers of a great-grandfather who took the Lord at his word that "his faithfulness continues through all generations" (Ps. 100:5).

My father was also one of those exceptional individuals for whom tragedy and loss never diminish their positive perspective, deep faith, engaging humour, and gracious spirit. Dad made it easy for me to think of God as a loving father because he lived all week what he preached on Sunday. Secure in the Lord and in himself, Dad was open to any and all questions about faith, instilling a confidence that God is greater than any question we may have.

A few years ago, I was asked to speak about what grace means to me. Immediately, I was drawn back to a moment when I was six or seven. Upset with Dad for not letting me do something, I went to my room, took a piece of paper, and printed in big letters, "I never want to speak to you again!" I taped it to the door and waited. After a while, I heard footsteps approaching the door, then what sounded like a little rustling of paper, and then someone leaving. Curious, I opened the door to read under my big printing, "Then that would be my loss. Love, Dad." I will never forget the impact of those few words. Dad had every right to be upset with this not normally petulant child. However justified, discipline would never have led to that life and leadership lesson on the power of grace—that grace always transforms.

Serving in a large downtown church, Dad and Mom made a habit of stationing themselves at the back entrance of the church after every service to ensure they met any visitors. Newcomers were often invited home for lunch. One morning after the service, I was walking by my parents with a group of friends when Dad called me over to introduce me to a couple who were visiting. Dismissively, I told him I didn't have time. Clearly irritated on the drive home, Dad simply said, "You are never too busy to be respectful." Another important life and character lesson learned in a few words.

Dad's faith transcended denominational boundaries to embrace all who claimed the name of Jesus. He had the rare ability to hold to his convictions while always showing respect for others. With a great sense of humour, he appreciated vibrant discussion and taught us never to fear people or beliefs that were different but to be well informed in shaping our own positions.

For some, growing up in a faith-rich environment, particularly a pastor's family, is not always conducive to a personal relationship with Jesus Christ as Lord and Saviour. My experience was quite the opposite. From my earliest memory, I have been aware of God as my Father and Jesus as a loving Saviour who is the way, the truth, and the life. Two distinct memories stand out: walking to kindergarten in Burlington, Ontario, while talking to God, and preparing simple little messages to share the good news with others. I smile as I recall preparing to share the life-transforming good news should a burglar break into our house when I was there!

At eight years of age, I committed myself heart and soul to the Lord in response to a Billy Graham movie shown in our church one Sunday evening. Sitting alone in the back pew, I was poised and excited to go forward, but there was no altar call that evening—something I teased Dad about for years.

I was determined that if faith was to be the foundation of my life, it had to be my own and not that of my parents or grandparents. I credit my parents for having the wisdom and restraint to allow me the freedom, challenge, and joy found in developing an intimate relationship with the Lord through all the circumstances of life; and many of the most challenging were yet to come.

SEEDS OF LEADERSHIP

Both Dad and Mom had a keen interest in current events, the impact of government at every level, and politics in general. With their non-partisan perspective, elections were times for lively discussion and weighing the attributes of candidates relative to issues of the time.

My father was always invited to attend the opening of the Manitoba legislature. Mom, who was working full time, believed it was important that I go in her stead, even though it meant missing a day of high school. I will never forget the impact of attending that first time. The pomp and circumstance were stirring, of course, but more than that, I had a profound but fleeting sense that this was a sacred event, significant to God and his purposes. The Lord was planting seeds that would spring to life decades later when he would give the vision that would blossom into the ministry of Nation At Prayer.

It is a moving experience now to sit in that same chamber and reflect on my very first time there, with wonder at the Lord's leading. How grateful I am for Mom's generosity to allow me to go in her place, an opportunity pivotal to my development in ways she never knew. That was only one of many times.

It was through anything but my own initiative that my public speaking journey began. From as far back as I can recall, I was volunteered or nominated for public speaking in all kinds of settings. One of the advantages of growing up in a pastor's family is that the church becomes like a second family. As a result, speaking in church or to church groups became quite comfortable. Additionally, through elementary, junior high, and particularly high school, I was increasingly involved in public speaking contests, usually initiated by my teachers, who would inform me after all was arranged that I would be presenting or competing. They would say they "saw potential," and I would say I saw "potential stress!"

Here again, pivotal to my development, Mom had great foresight in arranging weekly sessions with a renowned elocutionist. So, during grades 11 and 12, every Wednesday after school, I would stand by my teacher's fireplace, being tutored and critiqued in the delivery of different speeches and presentations. Over the years, I grew to appreciate what an invaluable gift this was. Far beyond winning competitions, it has been the gift that keeps on giving in leadership roles and certainly in ministry leadership.

Never sheltered from the challenges and realities of life, I am thankful to have grown up in a stimulating, challenging, encouraging environment with parents who were excellent models of character and faith yet who never tried to create a clone or smother their independent-minded and determined daughter. Having graduated from high school a month after my 17th birthday, I announced that I was planning to go to Calgary to attend a one-year residential program that focused on developing leadership skills integrated with faith, discipleship, and Bible study. It was a transformative year for me and the ideal preparation for university— and for life. I graduated when I was still 17, and I smile recalling how the residence supervisor reminded me with regularity that I was the youngest student they had had to that point, expressing it more as a challenge than as an achievement!

The Lord's game-changing opportunities so often come as unexpected quantum leaps. Blackaby, Blackaby, and King's insight in *Experiencing God* certainly resonates with me: "When God invites you to join Him in His work, He presents a God-sized assignment He wants you to accomplish. It will be obvious you can't do it on your own. If God doesn't help, you will fail."[20] From the beginning, my career journey certainly has borne witness to this. For a number of years I took the initiative in making career moves without actively seeking the Lord, but I was always aware of needing his wisdom and guidance to meet the challenges of each position. I marvel at his leading through all, whether or not I consulted him in the first place. I marvel even more at how he has woven every experience into the foundation for the next.

As a freshly minted graduate with a bachelor of education from the University of Calgary, I was offered a teaching role in Calgary in what was described as a "challenging situation." Excited about the opportunity to make a significant difference in young lives and minds, I soon discovered the full meaning of "challenging" as I entered a classroom of 39 grade 5 students, some of whom had significant behavioural or family issues. I grew to love my students, whom I continued to teach until the end of grade 6.

With a student-focused principal committed to academic excellence, teaching in Calgary was an incredible opportunity for the students and for me, so much so that we became a demonstration classroom for the University of Calgary and received special funding for innovative programming. The students responded beyond expectations and grew to love learning to the point that our principal of little faith would say, "When I walk into this classroom, I believe in miracles." One of my students completed a project on the comet Kohoutek that was deemed university level.

Then there was the Friday morning when I decided it would be great for all of us to get out into the community. So all 39 students and I explored the community, went downtown, toured city hall, even met the mayor, who stopped to engage with us! That day had a transformational impact

20. Henry T. Blackaby, Richard Blackaby, and Claude V. King, *Experiencing God* (Nashville: B&H Books, 2008), 208.

on the students individually and on our class as a whole. I also recall a very distressed principal on our return, impressing on me the importance of things like permission slips and advance notice. How thankful I am for the Lord's protection when I consider prospective liabilities or injuries. My first year of teaching was definitely a learning experience and never dull!

There were also heart-wrenching situations. One very thin girl arrived mid-winter with a dry slice of toast, wearing only shorts and a thin top. Her mother had been arrested for assaulting a police officer the day before. Another boy with significant behavioural issues said we were the first school to keep him for a full year. His family moved almost yearly for defaulting on the rent. A few years later, a candidate I was interviewing for a social work position referred to him as an example of her most challenging situation. Imagine my surprise—and hers—when we realized this was a student I also knew well.

As my grade 6 students graduated to grade 7 in junior high school, I was feeling a strong pull to move into social services. In accepting a position with Alberta Social Services and Community Health (ASSCH) in Edmonton, I had no idea how pivotal this move would be, personally as well as professionally.

Alberta was undergoing tremendous growth and prosperity under leaders who "understood the times" and knew what to do (1 Chron. 12:32). The public service was experiencing unprecedented challenges and opportunities, and professional advancement came rapidly. Starting in human resources (HR) as a recruitment specialist, I was ultimately given the responsibility to lead the first decentralized HR office, located in Calgary and serving a broad range of programs with over 1,500 employees throughout the southern half of the province. A tremendous opportunity professionally, it was a quantum leap in terms of leadership and impact.

A LIFE-ALTERING CHALLENGE

Thriving professionally in a role I loved, I was faced with an unexpected, life-altering health challenge. Advanced endometriosis led to four surgeries over two years, the last one being a complete hysterectomy to deal with advancing cancer. My high pain tolerance and long hours of work with extensive travel in a fulfilling role had worked against any focus on personal health.

It was the hysterectomy that finally got my attention. I so love children that it had never occurred to me that I would be unable to have any. To top it off, because of a shortage of beds in the acute care ward, I was given a bed in the maternity ward, just down from the nursery. How well I recall looking at those babies amid tears combined with wonder. There are times in my life that I can only describe as "the Lord taking over." To know that he knows our weaknesses and frailty is one thing; to live it is another of a whole different order that draws us deeper into him. By the second day after surgery, I found myself saying out loud, "Lord, if it is not for me to have my own children, I am trusting you to use me to impact the lives of other children." He has certainly kept that promise in wonderful ways!

The third day after surgery things took an unexpected turn. I had developed a serious infection and high fever. Immediately, a surgeon was called to perform a surgical procedure right in my room, and I was given an emergency blood transfusion. As medical staff were scurrying around, a woman from my church arrived with flowers. Seeing all the activity, she quickly left. That evening she joined a prayer meeting during which there was concerted prayer for me.

In the midst of the medical procedure, I had what can only be described as an out-of-body experience, looking down on everything going on in the room, including me lying there. Although it did not last long, it had a lasting impact. I remember an overwhelming sense of peace, that whether I was going to heaven or remaining on earth—either was absolutely fine. What I know is that when you die in the Lord, there is absolutely no fear. And when you don't fear death, you don't fear life.

The next day, my own specialist, not normally an emotive individual, greeted me joyfully, saying, "I am so glad to see you! Yesterday was quite a day—we almost lost you!" It had been quite a day, but in profound ways he never knew. My pastor called or visited daily after that; once he even arrived 20 minutes before a Sunday evening worship service. Recovering in record time, I was palpably aware of the incredible power of prayer and the powerful presence of the Lord.

The fourth day after surgery led to a significant awareness. I woke up with a strong desire to spend time with the Lord in his Word. At that time, I was not in the practice or discipline of daily Bible reading, and—unthinkable to me now—I had not even brought my Bible to the hospital. Bless the Gideons, who had put a Bible in the side table drawer! Opening it, I was immediately aware that when you are not spending time in the Word, you don't know where to turn at a particular time of need. As the Lord would have it, the Bible fell open at Philippians 4—there could not have been a more pertinent passage for that moment:

> Rejoice in the Lord always. I will say it again: Rejoice! ... The Lord is near. Do not be anxious about anything, but in every situation, by prayer and petition, with thanksgiving, present your requests to God. And the peace of God, which transcends all understanding, will guard your hearts and your minds in Christ Jesus ... I have learned the secret of being content in any and every situation ... I can do all this through him who gives me strength ... And my God will meet all your needs according to the riches of his glory in Christ Jesus. (Phil. 4:4–7, 12–13, 19)

There are times when God delivers us, and there are times when he walks through the challenge with us. This was certainly one of the latter times for me. The second Sunday after leaving hospital, I was anxious to attend a worship service. Still recovering, I chose to attend a church that was closer than my home church. Sitting in the pew, I suddenly realized it was Mother's Day; not only that, it was a dedication service for five infants. At one level, it was an emotionally overwhelming realization that I would never bear children; at a deeper level, it was one of my most intimate times with the Lord.

In her devotional book *All I Need*, Mary Morrison Suggs wrote, "Now I know that the purpose of all my experiences is to draw me to God, so that I will find His presence in my life a necessity."[21] I have come to believe that it is we who arbitrarily define experiences as good or bad. There is inherent value in every experience—if we turn it over to the Lord and allow him to redeem it. Even the most painful experience can then equip us to relate more fully to others and to be used as the Lord's instruments of transformation in the lives of others. The apostle Paul expressed it so

---

21. Mary Morrison Suggs, *All I Need: Meditations on the Master* (Ada: Revell Books, 2001), August 25 meditation.

well: "Praise be to the God and Father of our Lord Jesus Christ, the Father of compassion and the God of all comfort, who comforts us in all our troubles, so that we can comfort those in any trouble with the comfort we ourselves receive from God" (2 Cor. 1:3–4).

Infused into the essence of my being is Nehemiah 8:10: "the joy of the LORD is your strength." As a gift of the Spirit, the joy of the Lord is so far beyond superficial happiness that we need to take it seriously! In a fallen world, true joy is counterintuitive to our natural responses to life. It not only engages others; it is one of our deepest needs. There is no greater confirmation of this than that Jesus, in his final moments on earth, said, "Ask and you will receive, and your joy will be complete" (John 16:24).

LIFE CAN CHANGE IN AN INSTANT

With my health challenge long since past and thriving again in my role with the Alberta government, I could never have imagined that a scheduled one-hour meeting would lead to a lifelong commitment. In my capacity as head of HR and member of the Calgary regional management team, I was asked to a meeting by Mel Finlay from our head office.

Having only heard of Mel as a respected high-impact leader in ASSCH, I wasn't completely clear as to the real purpose of our meeting. As it would turn out, neither was Mel! He had planned to discuss in confidence his interest in the newly created position of regional director for the Calgary region. This was one of six new positions approved by the premier with overall executive responsibility for all social service and community health programs in a region. Mel thought my perspective on the region could be helpful. Also, I was the one member of the management team who would not report to the new regional director but would continue to report to head office in Edmonton.

As Mel walked through the door, it was love at first sight—for both of us! I didn't even believe in love at first sight up to that point. But it was real, powerful, and lasting (we have just celebrated our 36th wedding anniversary). However, at that first moment, I knew nothing about this man personally—about his faith, his values, his goals.

We did have the scheduled meeting, and Mel did become regional director.

A few days later, Mel called again to invite me for dinner, and I readily accepted. Never one to prolong things, I think it was between the appetizers and entree that I said to Mel, "My faith is very important to me. Are you a person of faith?" Imagine my surprise when he replied, "You could say that. I was ordained as a pastor and have a master of divinity." Imagine my greater surprise when I discovered that not only were his roots in the same denomination as mine but his family, upbringing, values, and faith mirrored mine in many ways. Within a year we were married!

Looking back at the speed of it all, we describe it as the Lord taking over to fast-track our relationship, not just for our great joy but for his greater purposes. We both marvel that for two independent and reasoned individuals on two purposeful career trajectories, from the beginning there was not a moment's hesitation for either of us. We could never have imagined all that lay ahead or where our lives would lead or the challenges we would face or all that God was calling us to. It was full steam ahead—and still is!

As an unwavering encourager, constructive challenger, and helpmate extraordinaire, Mel is God's loving gift to me. The one absolute for both of us is that the Lord is the foundation of our marriage. Everything, including each day, begins with him through time in prayer and in his Word. The Lord has often inspired or stimulated the solution to a particular situation through this practice. We have discovered that time spent with God is the key to a vibrant marriage, leadership journey, and life. The time available each morning may vary, but our emphasis and priority never do, no matter whether we are physically together or praying on our mobiles halfway around the globe.

Another significant and unexpected change came two years after we were married when we moved from Calgary to Toronto. Mel had accepted the position of executive director of the Children's Aid Society of Metro Toronto. Although leaving Alberta had never been in our minds, we believed this would be an excellent career move and an opportunity to be closer to my parents, who were living in London, Ontario. The month after we arrived, I was offered a contract with Kinark Child and Family Services (Kinark), the largest children's mental health service in Ontario. Little did I know what an incredible leadership journey was ahead with Kinark!

Change management was the constant of my HR career. My 10 years on the executive team came at a pivotal time for Kinark. In equal measure a profound challenge and opportunity, these years were underscored by incredible personal and professional growth. Kinark had 400 employees at the time in eight geographically dispersed programs, three of which were unionized under two different unions.

I arrived just after Kinark had come through an existential crisis related primarily to organizational, leadership, and fiscal management practices. With the appointment of a new board and redefined executive and management leadership, Kinark over time became a provider of choice for the provincial government ministry, an employer of choice, and a recognized leader in the field. To say that it was a lot of hard work by the whole team is an understatement of exponential proportion! However, I realized even then that rarely does an opportunity of that magnitude and scope come along: the opportunity to develop and guide a leading-edge leadership development program; to lead an "Inspiring Excellence" initiative across an organization; to be on an organization's structure, responsibility, and decision-making task force; to develop an innovative performance management program with a reward strategy linked with organizational outcomes (a first of its kind in the not-for-profit sector); and to lead the HR component of the acquisition and merger of two treatment agencies—to name just a few highlights.

During this time, Mel and I faced a significant personal challenge when Mel and the board of Children's Aid agreed that his contract as executive director would not be renewed. The months of his unemployment that followed were a time of considerable uncertainty and financial pressure. Certainly not a walk in the park, through this time we experienced blessings we never would have known otherwise. Oswald Chambers' phrase "the unsurpassed intimacy of tested faith"[22] describes beautifully what we learned and what it means to trust the Lord every day. By his grace, through it all we grew deeper in our relationship with him and with each other.

Although we believed that this was actually an opportunity and an optimum time for Mel to make a career transition, we could not foresee how dramatic—and how pivotal for the future—the transition would be. Over the incredible 20-year journey that followed, the Lord led Mel to specialize in individual and organizational transition, then to return to

---

22. Oswald Chambers, "The Unsurpassed Intimacy of Tested Faith," August 29 entry, in *My Utmost for His Highest* (New York: Dodd, Mead, 1935).

pastoral ministry, and ultimately to become co-national director of Nation At Prayer, which is his current role. All of his background and gifts are now used powerfully in our ministry to politicians.

IT'S HIS CALL

In my 10th year with Kinark, the Lord made clear that it was time for me to resign. As I was one of the longest-serving members of senior management, this came as quite a surprise to my colleagues. To finish well, to be fair to Kinark, and to allow some time to explore the Lord's leading, I gave four months' notice. I could never have anticipated how the Lord would use this period. Kinark was in another phase of organizational change, with a number of staff reassignments or terminations. As I met with individuals to discuss their changing circumstances, I was able to share that I, too, was leaving, uncertain as to a future position but confident I would be led to one. I was surprised at the positive impact of this, particularly when our leadership development consultant hosted a round table of women executives to hear my story of the empowerment of self-initiated career transition. A great opportunity, even as I was walking and seeking in trust!

I still marvel at the Lord's efficient leading through my four-month job search. The day after resigning, my first call was to the outplacement counsellor I had contracted for Kinark when we needed his services. I said, "Hi! I've quit my job!"

He replied, "Great! What do you want to do?" I told him I really didn't know but had always loved recruiting and believed it was the foundational function for any organization. "Have you thought of executive search? I think that would be a great fit for you," he said.

I told him that the idea resonated, but I really knew nothing about the field or the firms in it, let alone their reputations. "Whom would you suggest I speak with?" He gave me the names of the principal contacts in four firms and suggested whom to call first. There was my plan in one key call! One marvels at the economy of the Lord!

I quickly discovered that executive search was indeed a fit and where the Lord was leading me. So began a new and exciting eight-year chapter with Baker Harris & Partners (which became ATKearney Executive Search [Canada]). As a generalist firm, our work of recruiting senior executives for a broad range of multinational, public, and private corporations had tremendous scope, breadth, and depth. I loved and thrived in that role, working with stellar colleagues in a firm respected for its integrity and professionalism.

Working in executive search was a season of incredible leadership opportunity and blessing. During this time in my career, I received invitations to serve on the boards of World Vision Canada, Tyndale University College and Seminary, and Gardens for Life (Afghanistan); to become an Arrow Leadership Partner (mentor); and to become engaged in the developing prayer breakfast movement. What a rare privilege each of these has been, and how incredibly they have enriched my life, leadership, and faith! Although distinct in mission and scope, each was at a pivotal stage of development, providing the opportunity to witness first-hand the Lord's power to transform seemingly impossible situations when excellence in leadership is infused with deep faith and trust.

In so many ways, our move to Ontario proved to be more fulfilling than anything we could have imagined. However, only the Lord knew the full reason for our move. Almost one year to the date of our arrival in Toronto, Mom had a heart attack, suddenly passing into the presence of the Lord at the age of 66. I will be ever grateful for that one year with Mom and Dad after living three provinces apart for over 15 years. As Mom always appeared in excellent health, her passing was a shock and brought a deep sense of loss for Dad, me, and our family as a whole. I realized then why, six months earlier, I had been compelled to have a formal 40th anniversary celebration for Mom and Dad, rather than wait for their 50th. A wonderful highlight for them both, the opportunity to celebrate with members of their wedding party, family, and friends was a gift for which I'm deeply grateful. In all things the Lord is ahead, working for our good if we trust him!

Just over two years later, in 1988, Dad, as unexpectedly as Mom, had a heart attack and passed into the Lord's presence at the age of 71. It was a profound experience for my two brothers, Peter and Rob, Mel, and me to be with Dad as he took his final breath on earth and to witness his spirit leave his once robust body. Of course, for us it was a time of grief because Dad, like Mom, was a vibrant presence in our lives. But beyond that, his passing would be life transforming in ways I could never have imagined.

By Dad's hospital bed was his Bible. As we were about to leave, my brothers suggested that I have it. Moved at their thoughtfulness, I was full of gratitude. Having Dad's Bible in my possession meant so much to me, as God's Word dwelt in Dad so richly. I had no idea that in just a few minutes I would make a decision that would ultimately change the trajectory of our lives.

On the way home around midnight, deep in silent reflection, I made two key commitments to the Lord: to spend the first hour of every day with him and to read the Bible through every year. Even as I was making the commitment, I surprised myself, wondering how on earth I could honour it. I was still at Kinark with a schedule that was not quite 24-7 but almost, as we were in the midst of major organizational change. But a commitment is a commitment! And so, I just woke up an hour earlier each day.

How rich and essential that first hour of the day immediately became— and 30 years hence it still is! As the living Word of God, Scripture is Holy-Spirit infused, speaking freshly to what is needed for the day. During a time of great challenge and pressure, what a gift to experience the refreshment of the Holy Spirit in imparting everything needed for true transformational leadership—and the antidote to burnout.

TRUST AND TRANSFORMATION

In January 2003, after eight years with AT Kearney, I knew the Lord was calling me to make a change from both the firm and the position I so valued. Through prayer the Lord confirmed to both Mel and me that he was indeed calling me to make the change and to trust his leading, even though he hadn't revealed my next move. So the following week, to ensure I finished well, I resigned, effective the end of July.

At that time, Mel was the pastor of our church in Toronto. How grateful I am for a Spirit-led church family who live out what it is to love and trust the Lord. None of us at that point could envision how the Lord's call to me would impact all of us.

Almost three months after I tendered my resignation, on Saturday, April 26, 2003, everything changed. Early that morning I was reading 2 Chronicles, where King Solomon

> stood before the altar of the LORD ... and then knelt down before
> the whole assembly of Israel and spread out his hands toward

heaven. He said: "LORD, the God of Israel, there is no God like you in heaven or on earth—you who keep your covenant of love with your servants who continue wholeheartedly in your way." (6:12–14)

A few verses later, we read that when Solomon finished praying, the glory of the Lord so filled the temple that even the priests could not enter it.

As I looked up from the page, the Lord gave me a vision of elected leaders in Canada standing on Parliament Hill holding up the nation to the Lord in the name of Jesus Christ—and I could see Christians across the country holding up every elected representative in prayer. And, as they prayed, I could see the power of the Holy Spirit being poured into the hearts and minds of those who govern the nation.

The Lord was absolutely clear: this was not about issues; it was about the power and presence of the Holy Spirit in the lives of those who govern at every level of the nation. Then, as clearly and vividly as the vision, the Lord laid out the four foundational pillars for what quickly became Nation At Prayer: praying one-on-one with individual elected representatives; engaging the Christian community to pray for all elected representatives; sparking prayer breakfasts in communities across the nation; and resourcing others to pray for elected representatives and the nation.

Later that Saturday morning, when Mel returned from a men's breakfast at our church, he asked, "Anything new around here?" Still reflecting on all the Lord had revealed, I simply said, "I know what needs to happen in the country." As I shared the vision, Mel got it immediately. I've often reflected on how pivotal Mel's confirmation was—almost as pivotal as saying yes to the vision. The Lord is so gracious; he didn't say, "Go and found an organization." He simply revealed his desire and his heart. It's an organizational maxim that form follows function—mission and vision are foundational. And that is what the Lord gave. The form (structure) came later.

My resignation had come as a surprise to my AT Kearney colleagues. By the date I was to leave, the Lord had given the vision and mission for Nation At Prayer, which inspired some of my colleagues, even though it made little sense to them at the time. Fifteen years later, they continue to watch with interest infused with amazement.

An amazing journey indeed in ways only the Lord could lead! In April 2003, I could never have foreseen

- the keen desire for, and powerful impact of, prayer in the lives of elected representatives;
- witnessing the degree to which prayer refreshes, reinvigorates, and refocuses politicians;
- three MPs from different parties separately commenting on the same day, "Your presence is a reminder that we are about a higher calling";
- the ever-expanding openness to, and impact of, Nation At Prayer on Parliament Hill, across the nation, and amongst First Nations;
- the ever-increasing number of Christians passionate about praying for politicians;
- the burgeoning number of municipal prayer breakfasts, many serving as catalysts for spiritual renewal;
- a leadership role in a global initiative for Christian unity;
- the face of an eight-year-old boy excitedly reminding his father, "Dad, we forgot to pray for the mayor!"
- the Spirit-filled individuals of impact, stature, and deep faith who would serve on our board and in positions of leadership across the ministry.

Still fresh in my mind is an early morning meeting with a politician who began by describing his extreme mental and physical exhaustion. After our time of prayer, he looked up, saying, "I feel so refreshed! I can think clearly now." Only the Holy Spirit can provide that degree of refreshment.

Opportunities for a pivotal "yes" come to each one of us. How grateful I am for saying that "yes." Having faith doesn't mean there aren't times of uncertainty or experiencing a knot in the stomach—those times have been the Lord's gift in deepening trust in him. What a gift to live to the full what it means that as believers we always go into an unknown future with a known God!

Of course, life does not have only one pivotal "yes"—there are many, and we only know the full implications of our individual "yeses" in hindsight. If the Lord pulled back the veil and showed us the implications in advance, we might either be less likely to say yes or become impatient! It is always first and foremost about trusting him.

LEADERSHIP LESSONS I'VE LEARNED ALONG THE WAY

1. We Are Called First to God, Not to a Career or Position

Os Guinness in his excellent book *The Call* wrote,

> *Our primary calling as followers of Christ is by him, to him and for him.* First and foremost we are called to Someone (God) not something (such as motherhood, or politics, or teaching) ... Our secondary calling[s] ... are our personal answer to God ... Secondary callings matter, but only because the primary calling matters most.[23]

How often senior executives, leaders, and politicians spiral into an identity crisis of self-worth when their positions suddenly end! In a day and age of tenuous employment at every level, for believers two things are vital: that we never confuse who we are with what we do and that we take God at his word that we are created and always loved by him, we are his heirs, and he is always working for the good of those who love him and are called according to his purposes.

Os Guinness described life purpose in a way that is at once inspiring and profound:

> Our life-purpose therefore comes from two sources at once—who we are created to be and who we are called to be. Not only is this call of our Creator the source of the deepest self-discoveries and growth in life, it also gives our lives an inspiration and a dynamism that transforms them into an enterprise beyond any comparison.[24]

2. The Apostle Paul's Prescription

In his letter to the younger pastor Timothy, Paul wrote, "For the Spirit God gave us does not make us timid, but gives us power, love and self-discipline" (2 Tim. 1:7). What succinct and inspired wisdom about leadership!

---

23. Os Guinness, *The Call: Finding and Fulfilling the Central Purpose of Your Life*, revised and expanded 20th anniversary edition (Nashville: Thomas Nelson, 2018), 61.
24. Guinness, *The Call*, 22.

Leadership is about power and authority, for good or for ill. But when we invite the Spirit to inspire and infuse leadership, it is transforming. Still vivid in my mind is a chaotic executive meeting filled with blame and anger. Excusing myself, I went into an anteroom to ask the Lord to infuse the meeting and dispel the presence of the enemy. When I walked back into the meeting five minutes later, the CEO was apologizing to the team for the disruption and outburst. The transforming power of the Holy Spirit in the midst!

Leadership is about love. A wise friend and respected CEO so often reminds other leaders, "People won't care how much you know until they know how much you care." In our own strength, particularly in a challenging leadership role, we are not capable of loving all as God would have us love. We aren't—but the Holy Spirit is. He has promised us extraordinary power to love if we will claim it.

Leadership is about discipline—character, integrity, self-control. It is in this area that the most common derailers of leadership lie, for both men and women. In a blog post, Chuck Swindoll described four derailers that can easily bring down Christian leaders: silver, sex, sloth, and self.[25] Most leaders we know begin with the best of intentions for good—often in response to a calling. Over time, competing pressures, demanding schedules, mental and physical fatigue, and isolation can start to create vulnerability. While working in the executive search field, I was struck by how often executive profiles detailed superhuman competencies to meet the challenges confronting corporations. What Paul knew and passed along is that only the power of the Holy Spirit can refresh, augment, and sustain the leadership required to meet the challenges we face.

3. We Can't Expect from the World What Only God Can Give

As part of an innovative leadership and performance management program, I was asked to develop a benchmark profile of leadership excellence based on the three top-performing leaders in the organization. In addition to their individual leadership competencies, I discovered they had one very interesting quality in common: each was a person of deep Christian faith. When asked by the CEO about this, I postulated that faith gives the confidence necessary to step into the unknown to move an

---

25. Charles R. Swindoll, "Silver . . . Sloth . . . Self . . . Sex," *The Pastor's Blog*, last modified April 19, 2016, https://pastors.iflblog.com/2016/04/silver-sloth-self-sex/.

organization forward. Of course, top performers in an organization at a given point in time will not always be believers, but this was a compelling reminder of the power of faith.

A leadership consultant once wrote on the board "People Fail." A simple but profound reminder, particularly when we are so often surprised or disappointed by the inevitable limitations of people, institutions, society, and the world around. God alone, who knows the end from the beginning, is the source of perfect wisdom, truth, and everything else needed to enable us to meet the challenges of leadership. Only the power of the Holy Spirit can complete and transform our always insufficient capabilities. It is instructive that in Scripture it is most often those in leadership who remind themselves and others that the battle is the Lord's—not theirs. A confidence for all of us to imprint on our minds and hearts!

4. It's About the Questions
Impactful leaders ask penetrating questions. In reading the Gospels, I am struck by how often Jesus used questions to engage or teach; I am struck too by the brilliance of the questions themselves, which often transformed or redirected the conversation. In leadership, developing the ability to ask incisive questions is pivotal to making the right decisions.

Before every meeting, I pray, among other things, that the Lord will inspire the right questions—and I'm often amazed at the questions I hear myself ask and where they lead.

SERVANT SUSAN REPORTING FOR DUTY

One morning years ago, I jumped out of bed saying out loud, "Servant Susan, reporting for duty!" Mel, somewhat startled and bemused, said, "What a great way to frame the day!" I know in the depths of my spirit I am a daughter of the Most High, loved and chosen before the creation of the world. I know the wonder of his love, the riches of his grace, and "his incomparably great power for us who believe" (Eph. 1:19). As I move into each day, reporting for duty has become second nature. It is all about him, and whatever comes along he is there to guide, inspire, empower, and protect and, above all, to share the entire journey.

What an amazing journey it continues to be! How I look forward to all the Lord has in store as "I press on to take hold of that for which Christ Jesus took hold of me" (Phil. 3:12) in the confidence that the One who calls us is faithful, and he will do it (1 Thess. 5:24).

Living Faith on Fire

Wendy Hagar

Since 2003, a humanitarian aid worker named Carl Schroeder has taken a team from St. Catharines, Ontario, on an annual trip to Kenya to support their church's mission outreach. Sew on Fire (SOF), the humanitarian organization that I founded and now direct, has supplied hundreds of layettes to distribute to the women this group serves in Kenya. After each trip, Carl brings a team to Sew on Fire to help pack gift bags for others and share stories and pictures of their journey with our volunteers. On one occasion, Carl asked me if he had told us about the red layette.

I thought for a moment. It's rare for us to send a red layette, but I was interested. Usually our volunteers pack pink, blue, green, or yellow layettes and colour-coordinate them for either boys or girls. We display the layettes in clear plastic bags so recipients see all 25 items. The bags always receive a "wow" reaction from the recipients.

Carl described a scene from one of his recent trips to distribute layettes to a group of Kenyan women. He shared how the women held a baby in one arm and a layette in the other as they sang and danced in a circle, praising God for the wonderful gift.

As the women rejoiced, the team noticed one woman running away with her baby and the new gift. A couple from the team ran after her and found her sitting alone under a tree, opening her layette and trying clothes on her baby.

"Why did you run away?" one of them asked.

"I was afraid someone would steal the layette from me because it is so beautiful," she replied.

That is one of hundreds of melt-your-heart stories we are blessed to hear at SOF.

LIVING THE SCRIPTURES: LESSONS FROM MY PARENTS

For as long as I can remember, my family chose to follow Jesus. In Grenfell, Saskatchewan, our family of six lived just up the street from the little church where we attended three services a week. There were four Urschel children: Gerry (the oldest), Brenda, Wendy (that's me), and Perry (the "caboose").

Our household was always busy. On Saturday nights, Mom bathed us all, curled our hair, ironed and set out our clothes, and made Sunday dinner. For me, Saturday night was the last-ditch opportunity to memorize my Bible verse from the previous Sunday.

From a young age, I observed as my parents modelled the scriptural principles that would shape my future ministry. They led and trained their children in the way they should go (Prov. 22:6) and laid the foundation for the leadership I would have to demonstrate later to the hundreds of volunteers who pass through the doors at SOF.

One of the ways that my parents practised living the Scriptures was through generosity. Mom always passed down our clothing, winter coats, and boots to others in need. (How proud I was when I saw a favourite winter coat that no longer fit me on a little girl at school!)

Dad was always generous with his time and skills. I remember many times sitting in the car after Sunday night service during the harsh Saskatchewan winter, freezing, wanting to go home but waiting for Dad. He would be helping someone to start their car or to dig it out of the snow.

Waiting was hard, but it taught me a great lesson: every need is a calling. Whatever you need is in God's house! You don't necessarily need to pay for services. Someone in God's family has the gift or talent that you need and can offer it as a sacrifice unto the Lord. First Peter 4:10 says,

"Each of you should use whatever gift you have received to serve others, as faithful stewards of God's grace in its various forms." I take this principle very seriously at SOF today. Everyone has a gift, talent, or skill that can and should be used to serve others. At SOF, God has faithfully proven that this principle works.

My father also taught me a critical lesson about the power of prayer and trusting in the Lord. One day, while transferring a load of equipment at the Ontario and Manitoba border, my father froze his hands. Sioux Lookout specialists wanted to cut them both off. Dad walked out of the office, refusing to do that, and trusted the Lord to heal his black hands. We believed, the church prayed, and God healed. My father's example of trusting God and not giving up has provided strength and encouragement during the difficult times of my leadership journey.

HANDS-ON TRAINING FOR FUTURE LEADERSHIP

When I was eight years old, my father accepted a position with Trans Canada Pipelines, and the Urschel family moved to Ontario. Our little town of Ignace had 500 residents. To attend morning and evening church services, we drove 67 miles to Dryden every Sunday. Today I marvel at my parents' commitment to fellowship with other believers.

Because the distance was so great, my parents and the Groves family next door decided to hold their own Sunday school. On Saturday nights we rearranged the furniture in our home to accommodate our families and whoever came from the neighbourhood. As the work grew, we moved services to the public library, then to the Italian hall, and then to the school. I was asked to teach Sunday school at 12 years old. I was still young enough to be in a class myself, but I was needed, and the teaching was easy. I had heard the Bible stories for years. The truths were hidden in my heart.

Eventually, we purchased land to build our own Ignace Gospel Church. What a joy to have our own church and storage! Setting up and tearing down for church in the various locations had been hard, but it equipped me with the perseverance I needed to become a hands-on leader someday.

In our new church building, I was offered my own Sunday school classroom. I taught Sunday school throughout my teens. When I got my driver's licence at 16, my dad and I filled our cars with children and brought them to Sunday school every week. Our pastor always showed my classroom when he was giving a church tour because I kept it colourfully decorated and fun. I loved to fill the walls with God's Word and to display the crafts we made each week.

At 22, I found work as head ledger clerk in the warehouse office at Mattabi Mines, about an hour north of Ignace. My job was to help manage and maintain $20 million of inventory. Who would have guessed how indispensable that training would be for a future ministry?

While working at Mattabi Mines, I met an interesting young man. Jeff Hagar worked in the accounting department and came to the warehouse office to sort out accounting issues when they arose. I liked this guy! Mine workers could be very rough, especially with their language, but Jeff was different. He was raised Baptist and lived a godly lifestyle. He was the nicest guy I had ever met.

Within six months, Jeff asked me to marry him, and on June 30, 1979, we were married in Ignace Gospel Church. Matthew was born the year after we married, and two years later, Sarah Jane. We dedicated both children to the Lord in our lovely little church.

Life was idyllic in those days. Every Sunday after church, I made myself a cup of tea and phoned my mom. We'd spend an hour or two talking about the week and the children. I'd probe her about recipes: her sauces, Swedish *cumps* (potato dumplings), and mouth-watering treats, like her German chocolate cake with special chocolate icing. Little did I know how these special moments of connection and nurture would become embedded in my heart.

TRUSTING GOD THROUGH HARDSHIP

In 1985, while Jeff and I were living in Espanola, my mom suddenly experienced total kidney failure and multiple myeloma and had to be air-lifted to a hospital in Thunder Bay. Her stay there had some harrowing moments.

The doctor came into Mom's room one morning and said, "I hear we almost killed you last night." The nurse had tried to give Mom potassium pills. Had she glanced at Mom's chart on the foot of her bed, she would have seen the large letters across the page reading "NO POTASSIUM!" If it hadn't been for God's timing and my sister Brenda's intervention, Mom might have been forced to take the pills, and they would have killed her.

On my first visit with Mom after she was hospitalized, another incident of medical negligence occurred. A nurse came to give Mom a blood transfusion without running it through the dialysis machine, and Mom was infected with hepatitis.

When traumatic life events such as these occurred, our family turned to God. In late summer 1986, my brother Gerry went to Expo 86 in Vancouver, where *100 Huntley Street* had a pavilion. At the Pavilion of Promise, Gerry accepted an invitation from David Mainse to go for prayer and stood in proxy for Mom's healing. When David Mainse put his hands on Gerry and prayed for Mom, Gerry felt a hot rush through his body.

All of us were grieved to see Mom so ill and prayed for her healing. It was a Friday morning, and she was at the hospital. Routinely, the nurse first tested Mom's blood and then put her on the dialysis machine. This time, the nurse returned, saying she had to retake the blood sample. Soon after, she put Mom on the machine.

Five hours later, Mom was about to slip into the hallway washroom when she looked back to see a vision of Jesus standing with his arms outstretched in front of the double doors of the renal unit. "You never have to pass this way again!" he said. Mom was stunned and bewildered, not understanding his meaning.

Later that day, when Dad picked Gerry up from the airport, Gerry spoke of his experience in prayer that morning with David Mainse, but it wasn't until Monday's dialysis appointment that the effect became evident.

This time the doctor himself came to report to Mom on the blood test. "Viola!" he said. "You no longer need dialysis. One of your kidneys is working perfectly. In fact, you didn't need it Friday either. Your blood work was fine, but just to be safe, they did dialysis anyway."

Two years after Mom's kidney failure, one of her kidneys was healed! God healed her on that same Friday, probably at the exact moment that Gerry received prayer for her healing at the Pavilion of Promise.

Exodus 15:26 says, "I am the LORD, who heals you," and our family believed that Scripture. We were taught to trust God's Word by faith. His promises and his truths were rooted in our hearts. We believed Jesus could and would heal Mom. We knew his healing wasn't just for Bible days, because Hebrews 13:8 says, "Jesus Christ is the same yesterday and today and forever."

Sometimes we need our faith to be increased. Sometimes the faith of the one who is ill must increase. As we read God's Word over and over, we become convinced that Jesus can and does heal the sick still today.

TRUSTING GOD THROUGH TRAGEDY

In March 1989, Jeff came unannounced to my workplace. My boss said, "Jeff's here. You can go home early." I was puzzled.

When I got in the car, Jeff told me, "Gerry was killed today in a mining accident."

What? I couldn't fathom it! I was in shock. It couldn't be true! I believe I have a gift of faith, but I didn't even have a chance to pray for my brother or to see him one more time. He was gone. Just like that. A scoop tram had pushed him to his death in an underground mine, and he hadn't seen it coming. The accident devastated our family.

Tragedy struck again two months later, almost to the day. In May 1989, Mom was fatally overdosed at a hospital in Edmonton. We had believed in Mom's continued healing, but here we were, facing another shocking death. We were exhausted and overwhelmed with grief at the loss of two family members in eight weeks.

I can only say that we believe in a sovereign God. He chooses life and death, and as it says in Hebrews 9:27, "people are destined to die once, and after that to face judgment."

I have deeply missed my mom and our Sunday afternoon phone calls. For the next ten years, I would make a cup of tea every Sunday and think, "I should call Mom." My heart would sink as I remembered she was no longer with us.

A SEASON OF SERVICE AND LEARNING

In 1994, our family moved to Burlington, and for ten years I worked at the Western Ontario District of the Pentecostal Assemblies of Canada (PAOC), primarily in women's ministries. It was inspiring to work with the men and women in that office. Their examples of godly, Spirit-led, faith-filled leadership helped to shape my own leadership practices. I was also very active at our church, serving with women's ministries, kids' clubs, and Sunday school, while also helping to decorate the church for special holidays and events.

Whether serving in the PAOC office or organizing an event at church, I focused on developing a servant's heart. Leaders must have hands that are eager to serve and hearts that recognize the need to be constantly growing. We need to refine our leadership skills by turning to God's Word and by learning from the faithful leaders who are placed in our path by God. We are all a "work in progress." Our "yes" to growth, improvement, and new experiences unfolds God's plan for us.

HEARING GOD'S CALL

I have always believed that whatever we do should be as unto the Lord and that he should receive the glory. As a result, I always strive to do my best for him whether I'm getting paid for the work or not.

During Easter 1999, with Y2K approaching, I sought God to make sure I was doing what he wanted me to do in the Last Days. I undertook a 40-day fast to help ensure I was only taking on positions and jobs God had prepared for me.

On a wintry Sunday morning in February 2000, I was sitting in our church on a padded pew, comfortable, prayed up, preached up, and ready to be used by the Lord for his purposes.

On that particular Sunday, I listened to a missionary's story about an orphanage in Russia with 40 naked babies, and my heart wrenched. When it was time to support the missionary with an offering, I clearly heard the Holy Spirit say, "I'm requiring more of you in missions." God's voice was unmistakable and intended for me.

I froze. This was it—my valley of decision. How many times had I said, "Here I am, Lord, use me!"? Now, should I obey or ignore God's voice and run and hide?

If I were to obey, my life would change, but I couldn't imagine what that meant. What if God wanted to send me to Ethiopia? I did not want to go there! Regardless of what it meant, I reasoned, I had to say, "Yes, Lord, I'll do whatever you are leading me to do."

I remembered the Scripture "You did not choose me, but I chose you and appointed you so that you might go and bear fruit" (John 15:16). I was called, equipped, and commissioned by the King of kings and Lord of lords. There's no denying it. God had called me to be his ambassador and had authorized me for ministry. Matthew 28:18 states, "All authority in heaven and on earth has been given to me. "

I chose to listen and respond to God's call. Before the end of that day, I declared that I would clothe 100 babies by sewing pyjamas, knitting mittens, and making cloth bags, filling each of them with school supplies and personal hygiene items. I put it before the Lord. I believe God took those words, blessed them, and anointed the decision.

TRUSTING IN GOD'S ABUNDANT PROVISION

The next morning, I had a list in mind of what I needed to do. My first stop was to purchase material at Fabricland. The store was moving locations and had 75 percent off everything. I told everyone what I was doing, and my passion to help the orphanage spread throughout the store. The manager even gave me five huge bags of fleece pieces for making mittens. I marvelled at how God was providing everything I needed for my new ministry.

Even customers were curious, and some offered to help. One day, I picked up all the balls in a bin at a store. As I pondered the blessing one ball would be for 20 kids, a lady behind me asked sweetly, "Dear, can I have just one of those balls for my dog?"

"Oh, I'm so sorry," I exclaimed sincerely. "I need every one. In fact, I need a hundred of them." With enthusiasm, I told her about the pyjamas, mittens, and everything else.

Another customer in line overheard. "Can I help you?"

"I can sew," said a third woman. "I have a sewing machine you can have for your project."

I heard two other women talking: "Look at that lady buying all those T-shirts!"

"Who, me?" I laughed. They wanted to help sew and pack bags.

Our home became a manufacturing plant overnight as volunteers began to drop by with supplies and offers to help. It soon became obvious that God wanted me to clothe more than 100 babies! So, in February 2000, Sew on Fire was born. I was excited at the task ahead, and it didn't occur to me that I wasn't qualified to start a ministry: no degree, no Bible college background. Did I count the cost and stagger at the financial output? Did I make a budget? No! People ask, "How much have you invested personally in SOF?" I have to laugh and say, "I don't know. I don't even think Jeff knows. Only God does." I just did what was needed.

During the first year, people came to help on Mondays all day and on every weeknight. At 7:00 p.m. cars rolled into our court. It always overwhelmed me. I was so grateful for the help and support, knowing only God could stir people's hearts in that manner.

Margaret Gibb, a dear partner, came to SOF for the first time and said, "I feel like I'm walking on holy ground!" That is the way I feel most of the time, especially when I see how God opens the "windows of heaven" on us to pour out financial blessing. God has taught me that if you are faithful with little, he gives you much. His provision is steadfast and sure. I remember that as one visitor prayed for me, he said that God had given me the keys to heaven's warehouse. Those prophetic words foreshadowed the tremendous growth of SOF, fuelled by faith and the generosity of many people.

In the early years as I shared about the work of SOF, I was amazed by the generosity of many families. One family told me that their mission giving would only go to ministries that cared for widows and orphans. Perfect! Sew On Fire's theme verse is "Religion that God our Father accepts as pure and faultless is this: to look after orphans and widows in their distress and keep oneself from being polluted by the world" (James 1:27).

Another family gave me $500 for our work. Yet another decided to give $1,500 to SOF instead of spending it on Christmas gifts for their children (the children agreed too!). People were suddenly giving me everything. Anyone I spoke to felt moved to give. The seven rooms of our house and the double garage filled to the rafters, literally. I never imagined trying to grow the ministry, but it was need-driven, and I believe God expanded our borders as I proved faithful.

The intentional and sacrificial giving I have seen from people brings tears to my eyes. It always hurts a little to give because it is a sacrifice. Have you noticed how $20 seems huge when you donate it but so small when you go shopping?

Jack Hayford, in his book *The Key to Everything*, concluded that the greatest joy is in giving. Jack wrote, "our fears have taught us that to give *any*thing is to be left with less, and to give *every*thing is to be left with nothing."[26] He later explained that in fact the key to everything centres on giving. Through SOF, I have seen the joy of giving as a double blessing. Those who give are blessed, and those who receive are blessed. Our ministry is based on helping to equip mission teams so they can give and demonstrate the love of Jesus in a tangible way. This selfless giving through SOF is contagious.

ASKING BOLDLY

Sew on Fire has been the recipient of many unsolicited gifts, but there were also times when I had to learn to exercise boldness and a little tenacity to make a request. At these times, I drew strength from Scripture. In Deuteronomy 31:7, we read that after Moses called Joshua to lead the Israelites to the Promised Land, he told him to be strong and courageous. In Joshua 1, God repeatedly told Joshua, "I will be with you" and "be strong and courageous."

I've learned not to fear asking. What's the worst that can happen? I can be refused, but I'm not afraid of a "no." Usually before I ask, I pray. I first ask the Lord to point me to the right person and to prepare his or her heart. Even if the person's answer is no, I ask God to bless them anyway. If my request is rejected, I reason that at the very least I have shared my story with someone and possibly moved them to say yes next time. Secretly, I think when someone says no they miss out on God's blessing because my request is not for myself but to fill a great need God has shown me.

Once at a discount store, I saw many items I needed. The storekeeper said, "Great! Buy them!" I told him that I didn't have the money just then but that I would "buy by faith."

"What? How does that work?" he queried.

I described the need, the work of SOF, and how people give. The result? When I left the store, my car was full! I cried tears of joy at God's goodness all the way home.

---

26. Jack Hayford, *The Key to Everything: Experience the Freedom to Discover God's Purpose* (Lake Mary: Charisma Media, 2015), 18.

LEARNING TO EDUCATE AND MOTIVATE

News of the ministry spread. Many people from Canadian communities like Orangeville, Orillia, St. Catharines, Grassy Plains, and Deer Lake became contributors. In 2002, my sister Brenda started a branch of SOF in Sherwood Park, Alberta. During a 12-day visit with Brenda, I was booked for 10 speaking engagements to share about SOF. As a result, people dropped off donations at Brenda's house until they filled her three-car garage. For 10 years, volunteers at her house helped pack over 10,000 gift bags that were delivered to the poor in 20 countries.

Much later, in 2011, Bev Powell of Blenheim, Ontario, launched a branch of SOF at her church. In an article that appeared in PAOC'S *50 Plus Contact* magazine in October 2013, Bev said,

> In May of 2011 something wonderful happened as a result of Wendy coming to speak to our Women's Connection monthly meeting. Because of the overflowing enthusiasm that resulted, I spoke to a group of our women about beginning a branch of SOF right here in Blenheim. This idea was met with shouts of joy, and I began "SOF, Blenheim" with Wendy's support and blessing. I was ecstatic; my dream and passion was being fulfilled.[27]

Educating and motivating people became one of my leadership roles. Whether it was sharing the SOF story at a church or enlarging the worldview of our volunteers, I found joy in inspiring others by sharing what I had learned and lighting a spark in those who wanted to contribute to God's kingdom yet had lost purpose or felt they weren't gifted. The truth is that God has given each of us gifts with which to serve and bless others and bring him glory.

To help our volunteers recognize the needs around us, I would regularly invite missionaries to share stories of how the SOF packages were distributed. As the volunteers learned about the end result of their hard work, they were inspired and motivated. One volunteer said, "It was especially gratifying to see the photos and hear the stories of those who we sent packages to. Those beautiful smiles were so inspiring." Everyone at SOF learns how to initiate change with one small item at a time. This is a powerful life lesson.

27. Beverley Powell, "Don't Throw Away Your Dreams," *50 Plus Contact* (October 2013), 8–9.

ACCEPTING GOD'S GREATER VISION

By 2002, two years after me being commissioned by God, SOF had taken up full residence in our home. People advised, "Wendy, you need a warehouse. You can't live like this. Your house is full." I thought we were fine because we had always wanted to use our home for God's honour and glory. "Anyway," I said, "this is just for a season."

I didn't want a warehouse, but Brenda and many others prayed for one. Eventually, I too became convinced that we had outgrown our home. I accepted the fact that God had a greater vision for this ministry—greater than my home could handle!

Around that time, I gave a tour of our operation to Jack Hawkins and Sandro DiSabatino of Crossroads Christian Communications. They were amazed. Shortly after, Jack and Cal Bombay (who was in charge of Crossroad's Relief and Development at the time) invited us to share Crossroad's warehouse on Harrington Court. It was a wonderful offer that enlarged our territory, giving us 1,000 square feet for free from 2002 to 2007. With the large receiving doors, we able to accept generous donations from companies. It was a blessed time, for which we were extremely grateful.

CARING FOR THE ONES YOU LEAD

I never have to convince anyone to help at SOF. Instead, I tell people stories about what we do and allow God to stir their hearts. The result has been amazing! God has always been faithful to provide the helping hands needed to complete every order. Helping others to catch the vision of the ministry is one of the most fun and exciting aspects of my leadership role.

However, organizing the hundreds of volunteers who assist us at SOF is no easy task. As groups came to help, I learned to be more organized and to ensure that everyone was operating within their skillset and gifting. It didn't take long to realize that volunteers are more productive and the hours fly by more quickly when people are doing work that they love and having fun.

I could keep up to 70 volunteers busy assembling layettes, filling candy bags, sorting hygiene items, and more. The jobs assigned to the volunteers depended on their abilities and talents. Sometimes we packed 500 to 1,000 bags in an evening, but many times I would join two loyal volunteers—Evelyn and Heather—to complete orders, and we would pack 100 or more bags ourselves.

I believe that leaders should lead by example. Whatever we do, we must do our best and do it as unto the Lord. It's an act of worship! They say that *leading is serving*. I believe *serving is leading*. I don't sit at a desk. I work hands-on alongside everyone else. When leaders have a servant's heart, the people who are following are often willing to help reach the goal, even if it sometimes means sacrifice.

Someone once said, "Volunteers aren't paid, not because they're worthless, but because they're priceless!" I hold these words close to my heart! I consider it a great responsibility to love and care for the amazing volunteers at SOF. I have countless memories of packing bags around the table with volunteers, sharing encouraging stories, and praying for the recipients. Sometimes the volunteers themselves ask for prayer. What a privilege! "Let's pray right now," I say, having learned to cast the care of it onto the Lord immediately.

OVERCOMING GENDER STEREOTYPES

Today, in the 21st century, women in leadership face many challenges. Some of these challenges are for no other reason than that we're women. As a female leader, I have been ridiculed, mocked, and sloughed off. Such expressions of disrespect are not the norm, but I have encountered them more often than I wish to express. I recognize it's unusual for a female to be running a shipping and receiving warehouse, but people who are making deliveries are often shocked to encounter me, the *woman* in charge.

One time I met a driver who was making a delivery and reached out for the paperwork. He didn't glance at me; his eyes were scanning elsewhere. He needed a signature but really didn't expect to receive it from a woman when there was a crew of men around. Finally, someone said, "Give it to Wendy. She runs this place!" I have to laugh it off, but it's hurtful and hard.

When SOF required a forklift, I found one, visited the seller, received the training, took the forklift for a test drive, and purchased it. When it was delivered, the driver backed up to the door. With help, I put down our dock plate.

The driver came in and said, "Now, who's going to drive the forklift off the truck?"

I reached for the keys he held out, but he pulled his hand away, turning instead to Paul, a senior volunteer. "I've never driven a forklift," Paul said. "Don't give it to me."

He then turned to my son, who shook his head and said, "No, thank you."

Still ignoring me, he tried to give to the keys to a 17-year-old student.

I felt hurt and, by that time, angry. "You know, I sourced out this forklift, I test drove it, I trained on it, and paid for it. Guess what? I'm the one driving it, thank you! Please give me the keys."

People in leadership generally can be targets for criticism, but especially women. You may be familiar with the expression "It's impossible not to be offended; therefore don't take offence." I have learned through my experience that I don't have to defend myself. Rather, by grace I choose to place my identity in Christ, take the higher road, and move on.

WITNESSING THROUGH ACTION

"Don't mention your faith" was the last-minute instruction I received from a local college before I shared about SOF at their staff back-to-school event at the Mississauga Convention Centre. They had asked SOF to prepare a work project for 900 people to do in 20 minutes as part of the program. Daunting? Of course I said, "Yes!"

I prepared a plan of what the project might involve and presented it to the events committee. At the centre, we can pack 100 bags in 20 minutes with 20 people, so I reasoned we could pack 10,000 bags in 20 minutes with 900 people. Undoubtedly, a Guinness World Records event! The committee accepted.

It was very exciting and extremely rewarding to meet this challenge. The missionary William Carey once said, "Expect great things from God; attempt great things for God!" These words were running through my mind as I planned and prepared for the gigantic work project.

A volunteer, Teresa, helped me organize and compile all the supplies, colour-code the boxes, and pack the boxes on skids. At the college, we followed our floor plan and arranged work stations.

At first it troubled me that I couldn't mention my faith, but then I reflected, "Isn't it true that caring for the poor is actually a core belief that unites most faiths?" I was given five minutes to introduce SOF and instruct the participants on how to proceed. I gave a passionate generic description of SOF, our successes, our small beginnings, and how it's our desire that every child has an opportunity to go to school. The audience was captivated. It seemed they couldn't believe what we had achieved through one ordinary woman. I wanted to shout, "But I'm a Christian! I couldn't have done it without my God!"

"So, would you help me today to pack these bags?" I asked. "Instructions are on each table. Let's get to work and make a difference for 10,000 of the world's poor." The timer was set, and everyone worked.

The excitement in the room was electric. We nearly completed the goal, packing about 9,500 bags. The communications department put out a favourable news release on our event to the media, and it was picked up by several newspapers.

I learned later that this event garnered the highest participant survey rating of any at the college, and it was considered the best event staged because it held purpose for all.

MOVING FORWARD WITH FAITH

My heart dropped when I first heard that Crossroads would be closing their Harrington Court Global Activity Centre. Their lease was up, and they intended to move the warehouse to Circle Square Ranch near Brantford, Ontario. What would that mean for our ministry? Crossroads had not yet made their intentions public, so it gave me time to seek the Lord for direction.

"Wendy, you've trusted in the Lord, but maybe this is the end of SOF," Jeff advised me. "You've worked hard for the last seven years. You've made a big difference around the world and have inspired people to get involved. Well done!"

I felt grieved. Could it really be the end? My heart was troubled, and I just couldn't accept that this would be the end of this ministry.

It was a great concern for me until one day a faithful volunteer came to the warehouse. She had just heard of Crossroads' plans, and as she walked toward me, we both started crying. But then she stopped. She had suddenly received a revelation and burst into laughter. "They're closing so you can expand and get your own warehouse," she said. "You'll be able to set your own hours then."

I began searching for another warehouse and pleading with God to give us space free of charge, but I looked at 60 warehouses, and a free one didn't turn up.

A year later, in September 2007, Jeff and I signed a lease on unit 4 at 975 Fraser Drive. At first, the owner didn't want a humanitarian group in his building, but I was persistent, and it paid off. The owner's attitude softened, and he agreed to give us a three-year lease. We have been a model tenant for this landlord for more than 10 years and have received much favour from him.

In our own Fraser Drive space, as a Canadian registered charity, we grew again, and in 2011 we moved to units 6 and 7 with 6,000 square feet. We added unit 8 (another 3,000 square feet) in September 2016. With three packed warehouse spaces and 15 work stations, we are equipped to fill 15 40-foot sea containers annually with tons of humanitarian aid for hospitals, schools, and orphanages. Each year our volunteers pack 20,000 gifts bags and we prepare about 100 shipments for about 37 of the 101 countries we have had the privilege to help since February 2000.

When my husband Jeff retired from his career in May 2012, I asked him, "What are you going to do with your time? Are you going to volunteer at SOF?"

"No, of course not!" he said, and we both laughed.

Throughout the years, Jeff has been 100 percent behind me and my vision, always supporting SOF financially and helping as required. Few men worked on a regular basis at SOF, but when Jeff retired and began coming regularly, others were attracted to come. Jeff works in every area at SOF—solving printing problems, taking out the garbage, helping with installations, and so much more. Every job is important and not beneath anyone. Volunteers see that Jeff and I don't just dictate. We work with everyone to complete the tasks.

I tell our volunteers, "We all get the same pay: treasures in heaven. Your cheque is in the mail," and we laugh.

Jesus, our example, showed humility through his actions. He came to serve and give his life as a ransom for all (1 Tim. 2:6). By washing his disciples' feet—the work of the lowest servant—Jesus showed us what we should do. He said, "I have set you an example that you should do as I have done for you" (John 13:15).

Through our work at SOF—our acts of love—we use what we have to serve the Lord and give to the world's poor. Not everyone who comes to SOF has that mindset, but as people leave the distribution centre, I see how their hearts are stirred. Love is seen through action. The joy of giving and the experience of serving cannot be duplicated.

God sees the beginning from the end. I'm glad I don't. Had I known the details of running this ministry—the sacrifice, blood, sweat, tears, hard manual labour, long hours, disrespect, responsibility of caring for and spending other peoples' money—I might have run, like Jonah. I might have thought I don't have what it takes. I wasn't seeking to start a ministry. I just wanted to do what God had prepared for me and to bring him glory through it, using my gifts for others.

I'll never forget the prophetic word a South African evangelist spoke over me. She saw me like a huge tree dripping with fruit and hundreds of women picking the fruit off my life. At the time, her words scared me a bit, but then I just laughed, thinking the prophecy was unlikely to happen. I know now if we stay close to God, there is an overflow of fruit in our lives. Today I see how God shaped me from childhood, using my gifts and experiences to love and serve him.

I believe SOF is the Father's heart for his people, and I am humbled that he has shown himself strong through me—an ordinary woman who trusts an extraordinary God.

I am often asked, "How long will you keep doing this ministry?"

I have to respond, "How long does one's calling last?"

I usually say, "Until Jesus comes back." As long as God is with me and going before me, blessing, equipping, enabling, and directing.

Leading Anchored in God's Love

Aileen van Ginkel

LOVED BY GOD

*K*nit one, purl one ... How different would I be if I didn't have such a strong sense of God's love for me? How has my awareness of God's love shaped my leadership? Knit one, purl one ...

When I was a very young girl, maybe three or four, my mother told me that the Lord Jesus loved me. I was ill in bed, likely due to the tonsillitis I frequently came down with. What Mom said gripped me deeply. I doubt it was the first time she had told me about God's love, but it was the first time that her words penetrated into my heart. Since then, I have always felt God's love for me. This truth was reinforced for me in a dream I had a few years ago about two angels who were examining my heart. One said, "This one is in pretty good shape for someone who's been on Planet Earth for over 50 years." The other replied, "That's because she believed at a very early age and has always continued to believe in our Lord's love for her."

I'm a knitter, and, while I often do the knit-and-Netflix thing, I enjoy the times when I knit in silence, allowing my hand activity to slow down my brain. It's a great aid to pondering—the weaving of thread through needles provides rich imagery for the tangles of life and the ways in which beauty can emerge from the snarls of a chaotic mess of wool. As I knit, I think about the usual things: How are the kids? What's on my grocery list? Where's the next meeting taking place, and what will I wear? But I also take time to reflect on who I am in God, what God is doing to bring some order and meaning into the everyday tangles in my life, and the bigger snarls in the world around me.

A few years ago I completed a questionnaire that assessed spiritual gifts and found that I scored highest on the gift of faith. I didn't pay too much attention to it at the time, but—*knit one, purl one*—maybe it's helpful after all to think about my faith in God as a spiritual gift. Faith is the most basic gift, of course, one that I share with billions of people over time and space, but perhaps there's also a kind of plus-factor that some people are given in order to serve in God's mission in particular ways.

I believe that my grandmother—Oma—had that same gift of faith. It must have been hugely helpful to her and others as she supported my grandfather in congregational ministry, first in the Netherlands and then in Canada. Those years in the Netherlands weren't easy: Oma faced many challenges starting married life during the Depression and raising seven children, one of whom was killed after wandering into a train crossing at three years of age. The following years of war and German occupation intensified the need for a deep faith. Oma held on to her beliefs as she helped a congregant family hide two young Jewish children; she kept her anxieties at bay while Opa, my grandfather, biked around villages with underground resistance material, using his *Kirche* (German for "church") status as cover; she allowed Opa to pull out the prohibited radio at night to listen to the news of coming liberation on BBC. How she must have celebrated with him when he had the chance to act as an interpreter for the Canadian army personnel who brought freedom to their corner of the country!

Starting over in Canada—the place my grandfather was determined to emigrate to—was no easy task. Oma's six children, whose ages ranged from 5 to 17, would have had pressing needs, but so did many others in the newly planted Christian Reformed Church congregation she and my grandfather served. I imagine Oma's gift of faith was passed on to many people, especially mothers who were dealing with daily challenges while aching with homesickness. It's likely that Oma's gift prompted her to help found and serve the Federation of Christian Reformed Ladies' Societies in Canada.

Knit one, purl one ... Oma, do you see the similarities between us? I too love to gather people into groups and help them to do more together than they can do alone. And, by the way, that knitting lesson you gave me so many years ago? It continues to bear fruit, although I'm not sure I'll ever be as fast at it as you were! Knit one, purl one ...

It seems I've inherited some of the herding instincts and organizational abilities that are needed to gather people together for effective learning and collaboration. Since my late 20s, I've been able to use these traits in my work with the Council of Christian Reformed Churches in Canada (CCRCC, 1986 to 1990) and The Evangelical Fellowship of Canada (EFC, 1989 to present).

I had been a member of the CCRCC's Committee for Contact with the Government (CCG) since 1983. I was part of a group of Christian Reformed folk drawn from across Canada to develop statements on current social issues. Drawing from our shared biblical and theological understanding, we addressed a variety of concerns ranging from matters like Sunday shopping and government-licensed gambling to nuclear disarmament and the Charlottetown Accord. When my daughter, Alison, was born in 1986, I took up a part-time role with the CCG as research and communications associate. This position, which I was able to fulfill from a home office, required research and writing that reflected the consensus that arose as the committee discussed our various subjects. A colleague likened my work to that of a mother hen: I loved to see people come together and, out of their individual gifts and resources, build something more than they could have asked or imagined.

One of my CCG responsibilities was to represent the CCRCC on the Social Action Commission of EFC, an organization that gathers denominations, ministry organizations, and higher education institutions for collaboration in ministry and greater impact in the public square. In 1989, Brian Stiller, EFC president at the time, asked me to take on added responsibilities in the area of public justice in education. What had been a volunteer position became a paid position—again part-time from home, which worked well, as my husband, Ed, and I were now also parents to our son Michael and would soon be welcoming our third child, Mark, into our family.

When I co-chaired the Social Action Commission of EFC in the late 1980s and into the '90s, now working with a wider range of traditions, I continued to help people from different parts of the evangelical family come to consensus on statements about social issues. Anabaptist, Baptist, Brethren, Pentecostal, and Reformed—all had riches to bring to the table. I marvelled at how we could, after much discussion, agree on statements on pornography, abortion, reproductive technologies, abuse of women and children, and more.

My work of facilitating fruitful conversation—helping to draw disparate thoughts into threads of themes and patterns that were woven into coherent statements—continued as I focused my work to support the EFC's Task Force on Education into the late 1990s. My work blossomed further when the EFC established a platform in the early 2000s to facilitate the formation and operation of several ministry networks and partnerships. While my attention was now drawn to helping leaders with ministry affinities discover and support projects that they could do better together than alone, the work of gathering people together and facilitating their conversation continued.

So—*knit one, purl one*—what does the work I've undertaken have to do with knowing that I'm loved by God? My core belief in God's love for me, charged with the gift of faith, expresses itself in a hopefulness that obstacles in the road will be overcome and relational turmoil will be resolved. I hope I've been able to express through who I am, more than through what I say, the firm belief that the God who loves all of us will never forsake us. And because of this rock-bottom certainty, what we have been called into by God will always bear some kind of fruit, even if it won't become evident until years later.

Of course, not all of the commissions, task forces, roundtables, networks, and partnerships that I've helped to facilitate have experienced only positive outcomes. Relationships that are built as people share their ministry hearts don't always sustain the test of time. Plans adopted with enthusiasm at a meeting aren't always carried through as people return to desks that have been piled up with new work while they were gone.

I've been dismissed as a Pollyanna at times—someone whose faith is seen as no more than a set of rose-tinted glasses that produce overly optimistic perspectives at best or annoying illusions at worst. Such misunderstandings of who I am are difficult for me to deal with; I'm not naturally a thick-skinned type of person. But because I can go back to the sources of my faith—God and God's love—I've been able to move on from those hurts. Never on my own, however. I've always needed the love of others in community to do so.

Knit one, purl one ... How grateful I am for God's love for me and the way my faith in that love makes a difference in my own life and in the lives of others. Knit one, purl one ...

LOVED IN COMMUNITY

Knit two, purl two—oops, missed a stitch ... Where would I be without my family and my friends, the different communities that I have belonged to over the years? How has their love shaped my leadership? Knit two, purl two—found that stitch ...

I was born the eldest in a family of four children. My younger brothers and sister are amazing and so precious to me now—more, I have to admit, than I thought they were when we were all living in the same home.

My father was a busy man. He was a civil engineer and took great pleasure working in the growing metropolis of the Greater Toronto Area—especially Mississauga and Brampton, although we lived in Rexdale, now part of the City of Toronto, until I was 18 years old. Many evenings Dad would return home from work, have his tea and cookie, followed by supper, and then go out again to some meeting or other. He was an elder in our church in Rexdale and chaired the board of Timothy Christian School, where I attended elementary school. Dad was also active on the boards of Salem Counselling Services (now Shalem Mental Health Network) and Holland Christian Homes in Brampton, where he now lives.

My mother was a busy woman, not only with looking after a growing household but also with church work of her own. She became the head counsellor in our congregational "Calvinettes club" and later gave district-wide leadership to this denominational-affiliated girls group. (I'm so glad the name changed to GEMS by the time my daughter, Alison, participated. How could young girls possibly be considered female versions of John Calvin?)

When I was in high school, Mom shifted her focus and resumed her premarital career as a bank teller. She later became director of the Telecare Centre in Brampton, demonstrating her strong organizational skills and, at the same time, her compassion for those who called the 24-hour help line in times of distress. Mom was an important role model for me; I had no doubt that I would be a busy mother like she was.

My extended family was also highly important to me. As the oldest grandchild on my mother's side, I grew to be very close to my grandparents and aunts and uncles. Although I could question my father's or mother's love after a scolding, I never doubted Opa's and Oma's love. In later years, Mom would tell me that I was the apple of Opa's eye; I'll never lose that wonderful sense of security in my grandparents' love.

I hope that I've woven the thread of security in family with Ed and our three children, Alison, Michael, and Mark. That thread was tested when Ed and I decided to move from Ontario to British Columbia so that Ed could take up a job in Vancouver. We moved back again to Ontario when Ed accepted a new position in Toronto. Our family had to work together to overcome the homesickness that came with each move, which affected our daughter especially. I'm proud of how Alison rallied. As she put down roots in new places by building strong friendships, she demonstrated the ties—grounded in God's love—that bind her generationally to Aaltje (her great-grandmother), Aleida (her grandmother), and Aileen (her mother). We have similar-sounding names for a reason!

Knit two, purl two—oops, missed a stitch. What about that church split I experienced during my youth? How did it affect me?

When I was growing up, the sense of security that I gained from my family was reinforced by the broader Christian Reformed community to which I belonged. From Timothy Christian School I went to Toronto District Christian High School in Woodbridge. Apart from kindergarten and a year of grade 13 at a public high school, I had little interaction beyond the Christian Reformed community. Home and school were knit together with church. Even though we as Dutch immigrants were less visible than other immigrant groups, we formed a subculture in Canada that gave me a sense of protection for many years.

Subcultures aren't always a good thing. Small differences can fester, especially in a community that is as charged with a sense of mission as mine was. Everyone in my subculture felt called to engage in the broader culture with the vision to witness to "Christ's lordship over all of life." Christian schools and universities, Christian labour associations, Christian farmers' organizations, Christian newspapers and publishing firms, Christian political action groups, Christian arts societies, Christian mental health agencies, and Christian retirement homes—all these were expressions of the impulse conveyed by Abraham Kuyper in the late 19th and early 20th century. Kuyper is quoted as saying, "There is not one thumbs-breadth in God's creation that Christ does not claim as his own."

Not everyone shared this vision. Dutch immigrants who had settled in the US a century earlier found the call to engage in the broader culture extremely strange. They preferred to focus on building up their local church, emphasizing the importance of maintaining Calvinist doctrine and church practices. The pastor who came to my church in the late 1960s was a fish in the wrong pond. What started out as minor church skirmishes became increasingly ugly. My father and others resigned from church council; we, along with others, received our membership papers in the mail and encountered a building with changed locks the following Sunday.

The conflict I witnessed in my church as a young teen didn't break my sense of God's love, but it shook my sense of being loved in community. Those of us who were kicked out of our church home formed a new congregation, one that was determined by God's grace to learn from the past and form better practices of church-life behaviour. We gave our new church the name "Fellowship" and by and large lived up to it.

Knit two, purl two—found that stitch! It's not a perfect fix; I can see where the repair was made. How different would my leadership focus be if I had not experienced fellowship after schism?

The blessings of a rebuilt community that I experienced in my teenage years extended into my experience of a closely-knit community of friends at Calvin College, the denominational institution in Grand Rapids, Michigan, that I attended after grade 13. I haven't maintained all of my friendships from earlier years but am so glad that some of them— going back to elementary and high school years—are still vibrant and increasingly meaningful the older I get.

Following graduation from Calvin College, I worked for Calvin as a Canadian admissions counsellor, visiting groups of (mostly Christian Reformed) high school students at points across the country to talk about Calvin College and interest them in enrolment. This promotional work bridged my role with Calvin to that of director of development, a position I took up with the Institute for Christian Studies (ICS) in 1982. Between the two jobs, however, I completed an master's degree in Canadian history at the University of Toronto. After I was accepted into U of T's PhD program, I decided to continue to work in higher education but in an administrative role at ICS rather than as an academic. Although I would likely have enjoyed classroom teaching immensely, I felt drawn to a more active, community-based means of making a difference in the world.

At ICS, I was often challenged to use the peacemaking skills I didn't even know I had at that point. The professors in this small graduate school were never known for mincing words. In fact, the church schism in Rexdale was due not only to the presence of an ill-fitting pastor but also to the often brash-sounding statements coming out of ICS and related groups. I couldn't do much to change these postures internally but was often called on to smooth the waters with our supporting constituency after troubling statements appeared in print.

Identifying connecting threads between seemingly contradictory ideas was something I did without thinking in my early work with ICS and denominational committees. When I moved into the larger orbit of Canadian evangelicalism, through the EFC, I continued to focus on drawing the connecting threads into agreed-upon statements. I realized a few years into my work with EFC that the statements themselves were not what excited me the most; I was inspired by the ways I saw people coming together in community. Where barriers had existed between different branches in the Christian family tree, new understanding was emerging. Where doubt that we could ever come together existed, hope and faith in rebuilt faith communities was blossoming.

Nowhere is this more exciting to me than in relation to the Roman Catholic Church in Canada. I've been so privileged to co-facilitate the Roman Catholic-Evangelical Dialogue with my counterparts in the Canadian Conference of Catholic Bishops. Since 2008, despite many changes in the composition of the dialogue (but always composed of six Evangelicals and six Roman Catholics), year after year I have experienced the joy in discovering that our hearts beat in similar ways. We come together around, in, and through our love for Jesus, and we envision how we might follow him into the world together. The Roman Catholic-Protestant schism in Canada is one that will require much more time to heal—an even longer time in other parts of the world—but I'm thrilled to be part of an effort to rebuild what has been broken and to experience with others the deep grounding that comes from being loved in community.

Knit two, purl two ... I'm grateful for the ways in which my determination to facilitate consensus and to act as a peacemaker is a strong thread running through my work. Knit two, purl two ...

INTENTIONALLY INTEGRATIVE

Knit one, knit two together ... How does God's love, expressed in part by loving and being loved in community, make a difference in my life? How does it go beyond me and my communities to make a difference in the broader world? Knit one, knit two together ...

"Intentionally integrative" is a term I recently picked up from a colleague as a way to avoid the jargon that comes with words like "holistic gospel." I agree that we don't want to use language that too quickly turns people away from invitations to collaborate, but I don't think I can ever give up on the understanding behind the words.

I learned very early on that Jesus loves me and that he is Lord of all parts of my life. An illustration my teacher used struck me deeply as a nine-year-old at Timothy Christian School. Miss Romkema was telling us that we should not keep our faith in Jesus separate from all of the other areas of our lives. She pointed to the card cabinet at the back of the room to drive home the point: we should not keep our faith in one drawer and the rest of our lives in the other drawers.

The idea of integrating all aspects of our lives and living them fully before God is one that is more important for me now than it was for me growing up. If I were to try to make strict separations between Sunday and the rest of the week, between areas of life that require obedience to God and areas that don't, I would be attempting an impossible bifurcation. I would be living a disintegrated life that would harm those around me and put my soul in jeopardy.

In the early 2000s, I worked closely with women in leadership through NextLEVEL Leadership and the Leading Women conferences (2002, 2004, 2006, and 2008). We spent a lot of time talking about integrative leadership, as well as work-life balance. We worried about taking time away from our families by working too hard outside the home, and we worried that by paying attention to family needs, we'd fall behind in our work. My husband set a good example for me in this regard. Although he travelled frequently for long stretches of time, when Ed was home, he was home—he rarely took work with him from his office. When we were on vacation, he'd leave his laptop behind. This kind of compartmentalization was a good thing for me to learn.

The question for me is not "How do I balance work and the rest of life?" It's rather a series of deeper questions: "How is what I'm doing here and now a way to follow Jesus into the world? Where is Jesus going before me, my family, and those I work with to bring about hope and transformation? By what means can I/we join him in his work of bringing all areas of our lives into reconciliation with the Father?" Knowing that Jesus is going before us into the world is an overwhelming, joyful prospect for me, one permeated with hope rooted in the One I follow, rather than in my own ways of following.

It's like the story in Narnia when Mr. Beaver is telling the children who've just entered this strange land that the witch's spell, intended to create eternal winter, is coming to an end because, he says, "Aslan is on the move."[28] I still get a thrill remembering this scene. Although I'm keenly aware of winter's hold on our place and time, I believe that God is on the move. In God's Spirit, we can see signs that spring is coming and line ourselves up with those signs. Discernment of God's movements in the world and in my own life is thus critical to my discipleship. Whole-life integration and discipleship characterizes my desire to work alongside Christians who want to be fully engaged in the world they live in rather than retreat from it into ghettos of some kind.

Knit one, knit two together ... What difference has being intentionally integrative made to my leadership roles? Knit one, knit two together ...

My faith in God's love has helped me to recognize that what seems like a dead-end or failure in my life can be made whole again. God is constantly at work to restore and renew what is broken in my personal life and also in the communities I serve. Most often the means of restoration and renewal that God chooses are relational. My attitude towards another person changes as I sense God's love for that person; I come to appreciate what I had feared earlier.

The community-building work I do is all about bringing together the pieces of what was once whole—not, however, with the goal to whitewash those pieces so that they'll all look the same. Being intentionally

---

28. C. S. Lewis, *The Lion, The Witch and The Wardrobe* (New York: Macmillan Publishing, 1970), 64.

integrative means paying attention to each part, giving it full respect, and not requiring it to be like all the others. In Christian communities, the glue that holds these different parts together is God's Spirit, binding all into one—not blending all into the same. The body imagery used by the apostle Paul (1 Cor. 12; Eph. 5) depicts beautifully what I try to attend to when facilitating group consensus: we are not all the same; we have different starting points, but we can come together around our common calling and common purposes.

"Low ego–high trust" is a phrase often used by my friends in young adult ministry. We need low ego–high trust postures to enable collaboration. My colleagues and I know that such postures don't come about on their own. They require intentionally integrating God's love into all aspects of who we are. This includes our personalities, which are often so strongly driven by our well-intentioned ministry goals that we ignore the relationships with others that need constant cultivation.

I've seen the difference it makes when we seek to humble ourselves in the presence of others. I've experienced the ways in which individual spirits, softened by God's Spirit, open up to new ways of being. One time in particular comes to mind: I was with a group of leaders who, despite their best partnering efforts, were becoming increasingly frustrated by frequent impasses in collaborative thinking and doing. One person suddenly called us to pray, not just in a perfunctory way but for the next two hours. We agreed to this, but soon after I noticed another person leaving the room. Thinking that he would have no part in this time of prayer, my heart sank. When he returned with a basin full of water and a towel over his arm, I understood: we were to bathe one another's feet as Jesus did with his disciples. The work we did following this special time of prayer was unprecedented. Our ideas flowed smoothly and our intentions wove together beautifully in ways they never had before.

Innovative thinking and breakthroughs in agreement come more easily when we intentionally integrate God's love for us and through us. This brings a challenge to develop collaborative approaches to learning and action. I want to get better each day at helping individuals in a group to, on the one hand, express who they are and what they bring to the table and, on the other hand, listen deeply to the others in the group who are doing the same thing.

Knit one, knit two together ... How is your Holy Spirit bringing us together? What patterns are we beginning to form with one another as we bring your love into all that we do? Knit one, knit two together ...

FACILITATIVE LEADERSHIP

Knit two, slip needle into thread below to make a stitch, knit to last two stiches, make stitch, knit two to end of row ... How does my facilitative leadership widen the conversation and broaden understanding? How is it even important? Knit two, make a stitch, repeat at end of row ...

I've learned a lot from community development practices in the work that I do. I was brought into a whole new understanding of how meetings could be conducted when I was introduced to such practices 30 years ago. It was an "aha" moment that shaped much of how I led from that point on. No longer would the loudest voice in the room set the course of decision-making. Neither would the meeting's outcome be shaped by the one who could make the most rational—or perhaps the most emotional— argument. Instead, as someone facilitated the means for everyone to speak in an orderly way, individual threads of conversation were woven into a consensual form of thinking, and the ownership of final decisions was shared by all participants. Well, most of them at least. After all, those who were used to dominating weren't as thrilled as those whose wisdom was usually overlooked.

The voices of women are usually the ones that are overlooked in meetings. A memory stands out for me: I had finished facilitating a session in a conference of about 100 people and then walked into the women's washroom. Standing by the sinks were the handful of women who were participating. They told me how overjoyed they were at their ability to speak into the conversation, even though some preferred to do that only in the small-group breakouts. I rejoiced with them! This was progress!

Learning how to facilitate conversation has allowed me to help others see the connections between disparate ideas. I have been able to help develop learning communities in new ways—not just as ends in themselves but as the grounds for working together in God's Kingdom.

When Gary Walsh served as EFC president in the late 1990s, he recognized the EFC's potential to provide a neutral platform on which ministry leaders could gather and explore answers to the question "What can we do better together than alone?" Gary encouraged me to take up training in partnering development, a specific form of community-building. We were able to bring together a wide variety of ministry practitioners to reflect on the common challenges they faced and to resource one another for more effective ministry.

Perhaps more important than ministry outcomes in the long run were the trusting relationships that developed between individuals who recognized kindred spirits in others whom they had known only by name. Such relationships came about as people spoke with one another and shared stories over meals about life in the trenches. The relationships became especially rich as we began to realize the importance of bringing prayer into the mix.

A turning point for me came on a day when my colleagues and I were busy making plans for a nation-wide collaborative effort to help congregations engage with their neighbourhoods. Halfway through the meeting, one person stopped us in our tracks, asking, "Is God in this?"

An odd question, I thought. Surely we're all prayerful individuals. At least, I hoped that the others in the room were prayerful, because I hadn't taken much time to pray that morning, especially not in relation to the specifics of the project we were planning. We had certainly asked God's blessing on the work of our hands at the beginning of the meeting, but my friend's question continued to bother me well past the end of the meeting. Did we really have assurance that God was leading us in this effort? How could we know?

I began to wonder how we could be more intentional about bringing prayer into our decision-making. In some of the meetings I facilitated, we'd stop to pray when we hit a road bump in our discussions. We would often gain some clarity after prayer, perhaps because our thoughts became more ordered and our emotional feathers were smoothed down. Communal prayer helped us in those times to stop feeling like we were running around in circles. But, I wondered, is there more to prayer in communal ministry than this?

Fuelled in part by the questions around leadership that some of us were asking—especially my friends in NextLEVEL Leadership and the organizers of the Leading Women conferences—I was drawn to consider how facilitative leadership could make a difference in churches and ministry organizations. That nagging question "Is God in this?" gave me my focus. While facilitative leadership was the means I would use to foster discernment of God's leading, collaboration became the goal. Was it possible, I wondered, to interweave communal discernment with strategic planning?

Bruce Clemenger, EFC's president since 2003, encouraged me to give it a try with the EFC staff. Our weekly staff devotions became times when we gathered around God's Word to discern God's will for our future work together. It soon became evident that for many staff, though not all, this practice helped us to integrate our faith and our work in exciting new ways. While prayer was already an important part of our lives, we had not fully considered whether God had something to say about our daily activities. How exciting it was for us to know that God cares even about the details of our work!

The more that I studied communal discernment practices through the DMin research project I was conducting, the more convinced I became that communal, Scripture-focused, and prayer-based practices of discernment are helpful in providing clarity and unity in decision-making or strategic planning. Even more important is the shared assurance that a group gets when they come together in prayer around Scripture to hear the voice of Jesus in their midst.

I've learned, however, that clarity, unity, and assurance don't always come easily. In recent years, I've been privileged to facilitate the interweaving of communal discernment practices with vision-casting or decision-making efforts in congregations and ministry organizations. I've noticed that in groups where the majority of participants do not have an individual practice of Scripture-focused, prayer-based discernment, the clarity and unity in thinking falters and assurance is half-hearted.

Readiness for communal discernment is a pressing need, as I've discovered alongside leaders who recognize the importance of facilitating communal prayer among their congregants or staff. I've spent significant amounts of time discussing this need with my friend Christine MacMillan.[29]

---

29. For more of Christine's story, see *Faith, Life and Leadership: 8 Canadian Women Tell Their Stories, Volume 1* (Castle Quay Books).

She shares my longing that Christians working together root their efforts in shared acknowledgement of Christ in our midst. We hope to address the spiritual barriers to following Jesus in community and the means to overcome them in a book we're writing together. We've realized that trust in the basic premise that God's voice can be heard by human beings is a starting point, and we've been encouraged to see that facilitating such trust comes with practice and a strong belief that the Holy Spirit is stirring up even those who put up barriers.

My work with the EFC allows me to spend time with many reflective ministry practitioners. I've learned so much from them about how we need to rethink approaches to how we "do church" and how we undertake mission and ministry in complex, changing times. They continue to challenge my thinking about God's mission in the world.

The effort to discern God's movements is something I'm able to do explicitly with Roman Catholic friends as well as Evangelical. This challenge is also real, although implicit only, in my work as co-chair of the Canadian Interfaith Conversation. What is God up to in bringing formerly disparate parts of the Christian family closer together? What does God intend by having Christians work closely with Jews, Muslims, Baha'is, and many others? I don't have clear answers to questions like these, but I'm grateful to be asking them alongside other discerning disciples of Jesus.

Knit two, slip needle into thread below to make a stitch, knit to last two stiches, make stitch, knit two to end of row ... Just how far do our conversations go, Lord? I need to discern your lead even as I lead others. Knit two, make a stitch, repeat at end of row ...

DISCERNING LEADERSHIP

Knit three, knit two together three times, yarn over six times ... You're bringing new elements into the pattern, Jesus. Where are you going with this? Knit three, knit two together three times, yarn over six times ...

My knitting patterns have become more complicated as my experience with holding tension (yes, a knitting term as well as a dialogical one!) grows. From a simple knit one, purl one pattern resulting in a lovely ribbed scarf, I've moved into patterns that have led to some beautiful outcomes—at least, my husband and children seem to enjoy the sweaters and afghans I've knit for them. But it's the sock pattern that fascinates me most: what woman sitting in front of a fire came up with the idea that decreasing stitches in a certain way would result in the heel of a sock? And who, I wonder, invented circular needles to make sock-knitting easier?

Perhaps I like knitting as much as I do because once I get the hang of a new pattern, it's very predictable. I can tell very clearly when I've succeeded and when I've messed up and need to "tink"—that's "knit" backwards—in order to return to where the mistake originated. But elements of discernment are still involved. Will the pattern work out right to the end? Do I have enough wool? Will it fit? (I learned the hard way when the sweater I knit for Ed drooped down near to his knees!)

It's God who weaves with us the patterns of our lives, often in complicated arrangements that involve other people. How blessed we are that God helps us to discern those patterns. When we work with them instead of against them, we relax into the repetition as well as the variations of the patterns. The yoke becomes easier, just as Jesus promised; the burden becomes lighter (Matt. 11:30). Using the words in Eugene Peterson's paraphrase of this passage, when we accept Jesus' invitation to walk with him and work with him, we will learn "the unforced rhythms of grace" (*The Message*).

Such a hard lesson to learn! I'm realizing that I just need to resign myself to having to learn it anew each day. My friend Gail Reid has been so helpful to me as I do so. I remember when she wrote the phrase "learn the unforced rhythms of grace" on the whiteboard in the little room at the EFC office that was used for informal staff prayer times before the start of the workday. Although Gail has since retired from the EFC and I now work out of a home office, Gail and I have kept up the practice of praying together in the morning by phone for almost eight years now. Together we've realized that as we pray, our perspective on the matters we're praying about changes. We start to see them differently—not from each other's vantage point, because when we're praying we're not discussing things with one another; we're sensing that Jesus is there with us, just as he promised (Matt. 18:20). Prayer helps us to discern new paths of understanding, which bring us to places of stillness and peace.

The challenge to me, as a leader in the context of changing ministry landscapes in Canada and around the world, is to offer a style of leadership that invites groups of people to listen for Jesus in their midst, even as they listen to one another. Facilitating conversation and collaboration is not enough if it doesn't include hearing and obeying Jesus' call to minister with him in the world around us.

We can do our best to lead on our own, but together with others we'll do much better. And it's in the "circles of intimacy," as Christine MacMillan calls them—those places where we can truly let down our guard and close the gaps we've created between ourselves and other people—that we gain the trust that's so necessary to collaborative ministry. Such trust is not primarily in other people but in the God who dwells among us and through whose Spirit we come into right relationship. I'm learning that it's in those circles, through Scripture and prayer, that we can best discern what God is saying to us as individuals and as a group.

Back to knit one, purl one ... Your love for me is where it all starts, dear God. Without it, I would not experience love in community, I would not be called into your reconciling ministry, I'd have no interest in facilitating conversation for missional engagement, and I'd have no loving voice to listen for alongside others. I'm grateful for all you've done in and through me and pray for that ongoing assurance that you are walking with me in all I do.

The Making of a Leader

Margaret Gibb

F*aith, Life and Leadership: 8 Canadian Women Tell Their Stories, Volume 2* is another opportunity to share the stories of key Canadian leaders and their leadership development journeys.

Leadership is much more than a title or position or even specific training. It is a lifelong development process, directed, often unknowingly to us, by the One who called the leader. We mustn't underestimate divine involvement in our birth, our early beginnings, and the years of processing that God uses to develop us into leaders. He is the author of our stories. We are co-authoring our stories with him. Our leadership development will be as distinct and unique as our physical formation and composition.

We are all "fearfully and wonderfully made"—physically, emotionally, intellectually, and spiritually. Our stories all reflect a creative God who does "immeasurably more than all we ask or imagine according to his power that is at work within us" (Eph. 3:20). That is precisely the purpose of this book: to showcase how God works uniquely in the lives of ordinary women.

UNDERSTANDING THE CALL OF GOD

In his best-selling book *The Purpose Driven Life*, Rick Warren wrote, "You were made *by* God and *for* God—and until you understand that, life will never make sense."[30] For the prophet Jeremiah, life started to make some sense when God clearly revealed that Jeremiah's birth, formation, and purpose were all part of a much bigger story. Jeremiah 1:4–5 says, "The word of the LORD came to me, saying, 'Before I formed you in the womb I knew you, before you were born I set you apart; I appointed you as a prophet to the nations.'"

Every word is important in Jeremiah's proclamation. There is a "before" in our lives. We think conception; God thinks family line and genealogy: "I was formed long ages ago, at the very beginning, when the world came to be. When there were no watery depths, I was given birth, when there were no springs overflowing with water" (Prov. 8:23). *The Message* describes God's generational work this way: "Generation after generation stands in awe of your work; each one tells stories of your mighty acts" (Ps. 145:4).

The formation in the womb is God's creativity at work. When God formed you, he created a unique person with a distinct combination of talent, ability, personality, background, and gifts. He also gave you a unique purpose, a God-appointed assignment. You were called in your mother's womb, though you likely didn't know it.

Our foundations were established not by our parents or our choosing but by God. Phil Munsey, senior pastor of Life Church in California, wrote, "You don't come *from* your parents; you come *through* your parents."[31] When we are born, why we are born, where we are born, to whom we are born, and even the era in which we are born are all part of an amazing creative process that gives greater meaning to life, our development, and our calling.

God's call is a powerful force in our lives. It has the power to reach into the deepest part of us and draw out our gifts, abilities, passions, and dreams. It has the ability to direct us toward a particular course of action. God's call will push us to next steps. All the good that God has placed in us can and should be released and developed in our leadership development story. Effective and great leaders have a deep sense of divine calling. "I know God has called me" is an empowering statement that secures our identity and provides an indestructible anchor.

---

30. Rick Warren, *The Purpose-Driven Life* (Grand Rapids: Zondervan, 2002), 19.
31. Phil Munsey, *Legacy Now* (Lake Mary: Charisma House, 2008), 73.

DEVELOPING AND BUILDING CHARACTER

Are we here on earth just to fulfill a calling, or is there more in the development process? Rest assured that there is more—much more! Developing a calling and building character run together like a train track. Both are at work at the same time.

Ephesians 2:10 tells us, "We are God's handiwork, created in Christ Jesus to do good works, which God prepared in advance for us to do." The handiwork in our development journey focuses more on character formation than on accomplishment. Achievement without character will ultimately miserably fail. Character building is at the heart and core of Christian leadership. Character with achievement will have impact and a legacy.

Author Jonathan David Golden wrote, "Who we are and what we do are woven together in the fabric of our callings."[32] The person and work of the Holy Spirit are the key to transformative and effective leadership development. In Christian leadership, there is no such thing as a self-made leader. Our development process needs to rely on and work in partnership with the Holy Spirit. The Holy Spirit is more than adequate to free us from the limitations of our past and present fears and to equip us to step out of the comfort zones we have created. The Holy Spirit, who is both teacher and lesson, will equip us to become what we are not yet but called by God to become.

The stories in this book reflect the reality of the Holy Spirit's work. All of the leaders who have shared their stories within these pages were progressively changed because of their reliance on the Holy Spirit. They would attest that listening to the Holy Spirit became imperative in their development.

Attitude is the key! Attitude is a mindset that determines our interpretation of and response to our circumstances. Proverbs 23:7 tells us, "As a man thinks in his heart, so is he." The way we think creates our attitudes. Attitudes, in turn, shape our emotions and govern our actions. Everything about us flows out of the way we think. It shapes who are we becoming and will determine whether or not we can fulfill our God-given potential and calling.

We have more power than we realize because of the power and presence of the Holy Spirit *in* us. To be a Christian leader is also to be

---

32. Jonathan David Golden, *Be You. Do Good: Having the Guts to Pursue What Makes You Come Alive* (Ada: Baker Books, 2016), 28.

a spiritual leader. Godly responses to life, circumstances, and people become the seedbed for healthier emotions and greater development as seasoned leaders. Leadership is character.

LEADERSHIP TESTS, SEASONS, AND PROCESSES

Many years ago, I heard seasoned global worker Deborah Sirjoosigh summarize the development process: "There is a plan that is moving us toward the fulfillment of purpose. In between the plan and purpose are tests, seasons, and processes." It's the processes, tests, and seasons—often seasons within a season—that we have trouble with. I did! Trying to make sense of waiting times, setbacks, unfair criticism, rejection, aloneness, and closed doors brought much frustration into my life. My prayer journals reveal the pain. We all like to know what is ahead of us. We don't like unknown surprises or unplanned happenings. We, in the West, detest waiting.

Are there tests in leadership development? Tests that are actually divinely positioned in our lives? Many books have been written on leadership development and its processes. One of the classics is *The Making of a Leader* by Dr. J. Robert Clinton. Dr. Clinton presents five leadership phases, and in each phase he identifies the tests leaders will face. Some of the areas of testing are integrity, obedience, applying God's Word, faithfulness, relational training, isolation, and conflict. While the development story of every leader will be unique, the processes and tests will have remarkable similarity.

Leadership development will never move in a straight line. Life is unpredictable and constantly changing and brings a host of challenges and tests. Being rock-solid faithful is a requirement and not an option. Faithfulness is foundational in development, vision implementation, and character building.

Challenges and adversity always reveal character. It's not so much what we go through; it's what we learn in the process. Leadership principles are learned best from life and its experiences. Leaders are students of life. They have to learn how to turn pain into wisdom. Faithfulness is like a teacher because it gives us stability to take a high road and learn.

One of the greatest leadership lessons I have learned is how to lead myself. The greatest form of leadership is leading oneself. We lead from what is within us and what we have learned in life. There is an entry to the call of God, that moment of "yes." There is also a long development process until you become your calling. Give it time.

MENTORING

As we process tests, seasons, and changes, we will need mentors! Church Father Augustine put it simply: "No one can walk without a guide." Life is a constant journey of I've-never-been-here-before experiences. Mentors come alongside and help people to believe in themselves. They instill hope and provide spiritual direction. They are a sounding board and help people reframe experiences, failures, and challenges into biblical and life principles. Mentors are encouragers.

Mentors are qualified by their ability to process life and its seasons in a positive, God-honouring way. Effective mentors have been trained not by a scripted program or a planned course but by life and their own relationship with Christ. Developing as a mentor requires the ability to discern negative voices, adjust perception, and discern motives and attitudes in others and within yourself. What they learn in life qualifies mentors to build into and invest in others.

Mentors are qualified to mentor because they have been through enough pain to know its value. The best mentoring comes from our own pain. John Henry Jowett expressed it well: "God does not comfort us to make us comfortable but to make us comforters."[33]

The basic teaching tool of mentors is their story. Our stories are sacred journeys to be valued and shared. Mentors continually help people to see how God is working in their lives. They do this best by telling their stories. Once you see God's activity in your life, you see God as able, powerful, faithful, true—a God of new mercies and unlimited grace. That knowledge must be shared and invested in others. Volumes 1 and 2 of *Faith, Life and Leadership: 8 Canadian Women Tell Their Stories* were born out of the understanding that stories are a powerful mentoring tool. Our stories define us and are a powerful investment in others on the journey.

Every mentor needs a mentor. You never outgrow the need of mentoring. No matter how much we have accomplished, no matter who we have become, there is always more. Potential is very different from experience. What one has already done is called experience. What one can

33. John Henry Jowett, quoted in Ron Rhodes, *The Key Ideas Bible Handbook* (Eugene: Harvest House Publishers, 2016), 298.

still do is called potential. Effective and seasoned mentors do not settle, because they know there is always more ahead. They too need mentoring because they continue to face an unknown future filled with I've-never-been-here-before places. Leaders mentor.

STRENGTHENING SPIRITUAL DISCIPLINES

Too often spiritual disciplines are intentionally minimized in leadership development in favour of more visible and measurable plans and outcomes. While there is much merit in goal setting and strategic planning in God's development system, growing in spiritual disciplines stands at the forefront.

Paul instructed his protégé Timothy, "I urge, then, first of all, that petitions, prayers, intercession and thanksgiving be made for all people" (1 Tim. 2:1). Every spiritual discipline is an invitation to grow, broaden, and develop. Long before prayer is a delight, it will be work. Long before Bible reading and reflection become a source of soul-filling and Holy Spirit empowerment, they will be a task. Before worship becomes a spontaneous response of gratitude and thankfulness, it will be reserved for one hour at church on Sunday.

Richard J. Foster, in his excellent book on prayer, wrote, "Real prayer comes not from gritting our teeth but from falling in love."[34] When a leader learns the importance of taking intentional time for soul care, a greater awareness of God's presence in daily life naturally develops. Prayer is interactive communication with God and ourselves. Prior to beginning to keep a prayer journal, years ago, I used prayer as a sounding board, praying largely "venting prayers" and boldly giving God my opinions on what should or shouldn't happen. I did all the talking with my list in hand, asking—no, *demanding*—that my needs be met. I slowly learned that by pausing and intentionally listening, I could hear deeply. I was reassured of God's promises, his care, his provision, and his direction.

I now believe that prayer is not only interactive communication with God, but it is also a way of gaining new perspective on a given situation and an opportunity to align ourselves to God's voice and leading. Effective prayer has everything to do with renewing the mind, reframing our

---

34. Richard J. Foster, *Prayer: Finding the Heart's True Home* (San Francisco: HarperCollins, 1992), 3.

circumstances, changing our attitudes from worry to worship, and seeing life from a 30,000-foot perceptive. Worship and an attitude of gratitude flow out of prayer. When there is gratitude in the heart, we see and think differently. Leaders model prayer!

MATURING THROUGH OFFENCES

Learning to grow and mature through criticism, rejection, offence, conflict, and, yes, even betrayal is part of the leadership development process. The only way to avoid criticism is to do nothing. Criticism and offences accompany leadership.

Leadership involves people. Ministry involves people. Any public work involves working with people. In leadership people are your main focus, not programs. Learning to love people, not just like them, will bring its own learning curve. The contributors to this volume of *Faith, Life and Leadership* were frankly honest about their learning curve with conflict and offences. What comes through in their stories is that the way a leader responds to criticism or offence creates the culture for the organization and their own development.

Learning to handle difficult people will be an ongoing process in leadership development. Maturing in this area of leadership requires leaders to always consider a person's heart before considering their attitudes and actions. When God looked for a king to replace Saul, he told the prophet Samuel, "The LORD does not look at the things people look at. People look at the outward appearance, but the LORD looks at the heart" (1 Sam. 16:7).

As leaders we first have to remember what could be going on in a person's life before judging attitudes and behaviour. We misjudge too quickly and can overact even quicker. Before jumping to any conclusions, consider, "How can I help this person under my care?" Thinking of the other person first is the godly way to deal with offence and criticism.

Leaders are learners and maintain a learning posture throughout their development. When dealing with criticism, we cannot ignore an opportunity to learn. Criticism can be a great teaching tool. There is always something to be learned from criticism. Marie Miller expressed it best in her story: "Despite these challenges, I have had to continue demonstrating an unwavering and relentless faith and adding to that faith, love."

LIVING AND LEAVING A LEGACY

While many leaders do not give much thought to leaving a legacy until much later in their development, it is today quickly becoming a defining view of how we should actually live our lives. For many years in our leadership development we focus on the outward signs of what we do, but God always focuses on the inward—what happens within us. It's called character building. It's interesting that the ancient Greeks believed that character is destiny.

Legacy means taking responsibility for our lives through self-leadership because who we will become will have an impact on future generations. No wonder the Bible includes this caution: "Above all else, guard your heart, for everything you do flows from it" (Prov. 4:23). Guarding your heart builds legacy.

Legacy-building is in itself a journey, and it starts much earlier in life than we realize. It's a building process that runs parallel to how we respond to life with its challenges and changes, its good and difficult times. The choices we make, the attitudes we assume, the character we build through life processes—all inform our legacy. Legacy is built from the inside out.

We are all living a legacy even as we develop as leaders. Leadership legacy has to do with investing in people, adding significance, mentoring, being an encourager, affirming and building leaders, and making a spiritual impact. We are writing legacy in our developing story, every day. What you believe is what you live and what you will leave. Growing in faith becomes the foundation of your leadership development and your legacy.

Each of the contributors in *Faith, Life and Leadership* are building and living a legacy that will have an impact for generations to come. And so are you! Join us, as together we continue to reach for the potential that still lies within us. No matter where you are in your leadership development, there is always more! For God is "able to do immeasurably more than all we ask or imagine, according to his power that is at work within us" (Eph. 3:20).

Margaret Gibb
Executive Director
Women Together
www.women-together.org
For more of Margaret's story, see *Faith, Life and Leadership: 8 Canadian Women Tell Their Stories, Volume 1* (Castle Quay Books).

About Women Together

In June 1998, Margaret Gibb was reading John Maxwell's book *Developing the Leaders Around You* when she stumbled upon a simple question: "What is your dream?" In the space provided in the book, Margaret wrote, "I dream of directing a worldwide ministry to women with retreats, leadership training, and conferences to mission areas, villages, towns, and cities." Putting those words to paper was a turning point for Margaret.

At the time, Margaret was working as a resource coordinator for Seniors for Seniors in Brandon, Manitoba. Life was full, and she couldn't imagine how her dream would materialize. But an opportunity came three years later that would move Margaret closer to her goal: she accepted an offer to serve as president of Women Alive, a Canadian ministry with a mission to equip and encourage Christian women to fulfill their God-given calling.

During her 10 years of leadership at Women Alive, Margaret solidified her calling to work with women. Under her leadership, the ministry grew and impacted thousands through conferences, publications, and training programs. But Margaret felt something was missing. She longed to reach women outside the borders of Canada.

A first-time visit to Africa in 2003 with a delegation from World Vision intensified Margaret's calling. Witnessing the effect of the HIV/AIDS on women and children changed Margaret forever. She knew that she would set foot in Africa again.

After the passing of her dear husband, Bob, in 2007, Margaret knew it was time for her to launch into something new. She envisioned teams of Canadian women—nurses, Bible teachers, doctors, and nutritionists—who could share their skills and experience with women in other countries by providing medical clinics, education, leadership training, skills development, and biblical instruction. Margaret resigned from Women Alive in 2010 to begin a new ministry—Women Together.

Women Together was approved as a charity in 2011 and has been growing ever since. Today, it is actively involved in nine nations, including Kenya, Uganda, Ukraine, Brazil, India, and the Philippines. Each year Women Together sends several teams of Canadian women abroad to provide health care training, wellness clinics, leadership conferences, and retreats. The ministry also runs an empowering scholarship program that enables Christian women in developing countries to receive either a BA, BTh, or MDiv from an accredited theological college or seminary.

Retreats and leadership schools are new forms of encouragement and empowerment for many women around the world. Women Together's Peer Care retreats and Connect Leadership schools have been welcomed in three nations. Peer Care retreats are intimate gatherings of women in leadership for a weekend of mentoring, prayer, and leadership lessons, while the Connect Leadership schools provide a three-day intensive Christian leadership training program in a conference-like setting. Both programs have been transformational.

Technology has helped Women Together to expand its reach. With the help of webinar technology, Margaret and her team have led dozens of leadership webinars that have enabled hundreds of women across the globe to receive outstanding Christian leadership training at no cost.

In Canada, Women Together is actively working to bring Christian women together for spiritual encouragement, mentoring, and leadership training. Recently, Women Together launched the National Prayer Network—a bi-monthly online prayer session that unites women in prayer all across Canada. Margaret and her team have also launched a three-day international leadership forum—*CALLED*—in Guelph, Ontario, that draws leaders from across Canada and as far away as Nepal and the Philippines. *CALLED* has affirmed that there is a hunger in Canada for multicultural and multigenerational Christian leadership training.

The book you are holding in your hands is another effort of Women Together to equip and empower women to fulfill their God-given calling. It is our hope that in this second volume of *Faith, Life, and Leadership*, the diverse stories of women stepping outside of their comfort zones to reach their God-given potential will inspire you to do the same. Ephesians 3:20 was and continues to be a strong motivator for Margaret Gibb and her team: God is "able to do immeasurably more than all we ask or imagine, according to his power that is at work within us." Amen. May you be released into the unimaginable journey that the Lord has set before you.

WOMEN TOGETHER

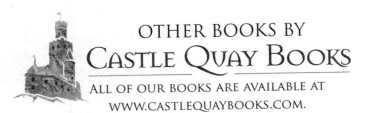

WINNER

CULTURE
BOOK OF
THE YEAR
2018

Faith,
LEADERSHIP
and Public Life

Leadership Lessons
from Moses to Jesus

Preston Manning

"Imagine a treasure box for leaders
with everything you could possibly need in it..."
from the foreword by Mark Buchanan

Leading Me

Eight Practices for a Christian Leader's
Most Important Assignment

Steve A. Brown

SHORTLIST

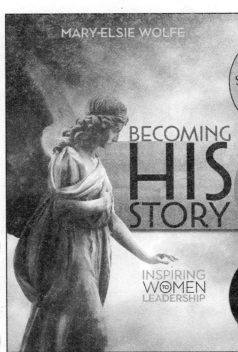

MARY-ELSIE WOLFE

BECOMING **HIS** STORY

INSPIRING WOMEN TO LEADERSHIP

BIBLICAL STUDIES BOOK OF THE YEAR 2018

CULTURE BOOK OF THE YEAR 2018

CHRISTIAN LIVING BOOK OF THE YEAR 2018

GRACE IRWIN BEST BOOK OF THE YEAR 2019

LIFE STORIES BOOK OF THE YEAR 2019

DEBORAH FIEGUTH'S SOCIAL JUSTICE AWARD 2019

THE **TRUE STORY** OF CANADIAN HUMAN TRAFFICKING

BY PAUL H. BOGE
FOREWORD BY PAUL BRANDT

WINNER